Definite Articles

How to Write and Sell Winning Articles Based on Your Overseas Experience

By Jo Parfitt

SUMMERTIME PUBLISHING

First published in 2003 by Summertime Publishing
Third edition 2010

Website: www.joparfitt.com

ISBN 9781904881339

Dedication

This course is not dedicated to my school careers advisor who once told me that writing was not a proper career. It is, instead, dedicated to all those people who have believed in me, every editor who has acknowledged his or her faith in my words by paying me real money for them and my students who have paid me the compliment of becoming real, published, writers after taking this course.

Acknowledgements

Many people have helped to turn this course into what it is today. My students have given me valuable feedback and it has only been by running this program both online and in live workshops that it has been able to develop into the e-course you now have before you.

More recently, I have to thank Christine Hayes, Renata Harper and Sam Parfitt for their constructive criticism and editing work and Creation Booth and Sam Parfitt for their work with design and layout.

Contents

Introduction

Writing is the perfect portable career. It is also an invaluable skill for anyone who requires an extra source of income or a hobby with earning potential. These days, so many people move around the country or the world, and live in places other than where they grew up. Their observations and experiences make great reading and are a constant source of inspiration. Through widespread TV ownership and Internet use, not to mention tourism on a grand scale, the world has become a global village. English may not be the language spoken by the greatest number of people in the world, but it almost certainly is the most *widespread* language. I have lived and worked abroad myself for over 20 years and though I have sold countless articles to national publications, much of my experience and contacts are international. This course is of particular interest to people who have had overseas experience, though it is in no way designed exclusively for expats. It is of use to anyone who has travelled or not, for the tools, tips and information are exactly the same. What makes this course of special use to expatriates is my own network of publications to whom I can introduce you during the course. That many examples are feminine in nature is because they come from my own experience. I have attempted to redress this balance by adding more male or unisex topics too. Indeed, just as you do not have to have lived overseas to benefit from this program, neither do you have to be female!

You don't have to be a prize-winning novelist to be a published writer. Writing for publication takes many forms, and you can make a career in writing wherever you may live, providing you have a computer and Internet connection. This course shows you where to get inspiration and how to turn those ideas into words that sell. You can easily create articles about what you know and who you know. You do not even need to do lots of extra research; all you need is the will to write and access to a little professional advice. Discover these secrets and more from a wordsmith who has been, variously, author, poet, short story writer, student, teacher, journalist, publisher, editor, presenter and copywriter. She has kept her career well and truly alive while living overseas, spending more than 20 years in five different countries.

This course will give you hands-on learning about far more than just the mechanics of writing. You will also learn how to find the markets that are out there and how to get editors to say "yes" to your manuscripts.

The author and tutor

I have been a journalist for over 20 years and have had hundreds of articles published all over the world in a wide variety of magazines, papers and websites. I have been published in newspapers, including *The Independent on Sunday*, *The European* and the *Weekly Telegraph*. In addition, I run my own publishing company, Summertime Publishing, and am perhaps best known for my *A Career in Your Suitcase* books. Between 1985 and 1992 I had more than 15 books published by major publishing companies. As editor of *Woman Abroad* magazine from 1999 to 2002, I discovered first hand what an editor was looking for and how it felt when the boot was on the other foot and it was my turn to commission writers. My work editing *Global Connection* and *Women's Business* magazines built on this knowledge and mean that I know what an editor wants. As a direct result, I can guide you towards becoming a successful contributor to the publications of your choice.

Work at your own pace

Working at your own pace has the advantage of letting you work round your holidays and other activities, and you can take as much time as you need to complete assignments.

Past students have given me permission to circulate some of their homework assignments, so you also get to review their work. This will inspire and empower you as you complete your own homework tasks.

You can start the course when you like.

All you have to do is complete the exercises in order, submitting each one after you have received the assessment for the previous assignment.

Work with a personal tutor

Definite Articles is more than a workbook because, although you can work with it alone, feedback is available via a personal tutor. There is an additional fee of €250 for this personal feedback. The course has been divided into eight sessions, each of which concludes with an exercise. Feedback is invaluable to the writer, but with *Definite Articles* you will find that some of your assignments may require extra attention and that there will occasionally be a series of emails about one piece of homework. This extra help is provided free of charge.

To book your personal tutor please send an email with the subject 'Personal Tutor for *Definite Articles*' to feedback@joparfitt.com. Then simply send each assignment by email to your personal tutor and it will be critiqued for you within two weeks of receipt.

Cost of working with a personal tutor   €250

And after the course

Once you have completed the eight assignments you have the chance to benefit from a six further months' of additional help, connections, editing, advice, critique and mentoring. During this period I will send you leads to commissions from editors with whom I have built a relationship specifically for the benefit of my students. You will receive at least one lead every month and will be able to have your ensuing pitches and articles checked before you send them off. In addition, you will be able to discuss any of your own ideas during this time.

Sign up for six months' of mentoring and you will receive:

1. Copies of at least three recently published books, ripe for review.
2. Connections to the authors of the new books, who will be delighted to be interviewed by you.
3. Review of up to one pitch per week.
4. Review of up to one article per week, to a maximum of 3,000 words per month.
5. Connections to editors who are looking for material as and when I hear of them (expect this to happen at least once a month). Right now I have a database of over 400 publications and I hear from my connections regularly.
6. The potential to have at least six pieces published during this period (if you follow my leads and advice and take action, that is!)
7. The six-month period commences on the day you receive your final piece of homework back from me, or the day payment is received for the mentoring, whichever comes later. It can be extended for a further six months if required.

Cost of six months' mentoring   €300

To sign up to work with a personal tutor or the mentoring program please email feedback@joparfitt.com.

I look forward to working with you.

Jo Parfitt

LESSON ONE

Finding Ideas

How many times have you been told that you should write about what you know? Well, as a published journalist with hundreds of articles printed and paid for, I agree wholeheartedly.

The best place to start your writing career *really is* by writing about what you know. That means writing about the people you have met, the places you have visited and the things you have learned.

Inspire yourself

Most of your best ideas will come from reflecting on who you are: your own experience and your take on what has happened to you and is happening around you. You are unique. Your personal viewpoint will add interest to stories that could otherwise be dull and boring.

Take me, for example. I have studied French, lived in London as a single girl, married someone I met at university, become a mother to two boys, lived in France, written two cookery books, run a restaurant, crashed the first car I drove, lost my job, found a job, began my own business in a foreign country, lived in the Middle East without learning Arabic and Norway without learning Norwegian, learned to dive, learned to drive on the right, learned to drive in sand dunes ...

I have met people who worked as potters, weavers, musicians, aerobics teachers, jewellery makers, homeopaths, volunteers and many more – and all have become the inspiration for articles that I have sold. When I lived in Oman I wrote for airline magazines that served the Middle East and sold stories about dates, spices, fish, water, local crafts and a range of other subjects specific to the area.

When I went back to live in England I wrote about repatriation, careers, house-buying, and all the people I stay in touch with all over the world. Today I live in Holland and have written about riding a bicycle, running a business in the Netherlands, learning to speak Dutch (yes, I have done that at last!) and so on.

Get the idea?

You can write about anything and everything. Who you know – some of your closest friends, new acquaintances or friends of friends could be the subjects of inspiring interviews. Ask yourself: if you were to read an article about a person, what you would like to know? Then it is up to YOU to write the article that interests you.

Who are you? Daughter, husband, parent, an elder sibling? A country girl, a beekeeper, an expatriate, a divorced person, an exercise enthusiast? Adding your own perspective to an article is what will help make an idea fresh and interesting.

What kinds of things have you done so far? Have you learned Spanish, conquered your fear of flying, backpacked around Bangladesh, bought silver in Oman, discovered a Bedouin tribe? Many of the things you have experienced will interest other people too.

Where have you been? Where have you lived, where have you travelled, where have you worked? All these details offer new angles; new perspectives that can make an old story come alive. Your experiences will differ according to your circumstances. A weekend visitor to Prague needs to know different things about the city than, say a businessman, or a family with young children.

What do you love? What are you passionate about? What really matters to you? What do you find yourself arguing about with friends or making a detour to see when you are on holiday? If you are passionate about something you are sure to be able to write about it.

What do you know? Have you studied anthropology, do you subscribe to a yachting magazine, and do you know how to build a glider, or cook without wheat? What courses have you taken – or given? What have you learned or researched? If the subject interests you it almost certainly will interest others, and there may even be a publication dedicated to the topic.

Consider

- Have you ever been in danger? Have you known anyone who has been in a dangerous situation? Any success stories? Sad stories?
- Has anything funny happened to you or a friend or relative? Could you write about it?
- Can you think of anything amusing about a familiar situation, such as shopping, Christmas, or holidays?
- Have you been to the theatre, cinema, a hypnotherapist, a lecture? Someone may like to learn from your experience.

> Anything that happens in your life could turn into a story
> – even the bad things.

Everyone you talk to, everything you hear, everything you read, every course you attend, every journey, holiday, experience (good and bad), could become a written story. Whenever something bad happens to me, I never fail to see the positive aspects of the situation. I know the event could become an article, so I make sure to write down how I am feeling, so that I can bring it all to life again later.

Once, in Oman, I found myself stranded in the middle of a roundabout when the car simply stopped. Soon, I was surrounded by police and concerned motorists. It transpired I had just run out of petrol. Rather than feeling a complete idiot I realised I had just been fed some rather good material for a humorous column about driving.

Things you can write

Here is a list of just some of the articles or short pieces you could write for publication.

Ideas

- letters to the editor
- interviews
- features
- reviews of books, plays, websites, events, restaurants
- beauty
- lifestyle
- fashion
- property
- education
- family
- spirituality
- psychology
- careers
- business
- self-development
- news and current affairs
- health
- fitness
- shopping
- fiction
- cookery

- product evaluation
- humour
- columns
- tips
- secrets
- how to …
- new research
- travel
- advertorial – it looks like an article but is actually an advert

Publications

Here is a list of some of the different types of publication you could be writing for:

- women's magazines
- men's magazines
- hobby magazines
- trade magazines
- in-flight magazines
- Sunday or other newspaper supplements
- local newspapers
- national newspapers
- international newspapers
- free papers
- in-store magazines
- travel brochures
- club, members' or network magazines
- what's on magazines
- company magazines
- local interest magazines
- brochures
- websites
- newsletters

Writing about yourself

To begin with, most of your inspiration will come from things that have happened to you. So, you have bought a new house in the Middle East and offer a piece on this subject to a property paper. In this case you can either include your own experience in the story (making it personal) or exclude your story (making it objective). The fact that you have first hand experience of doing this too, gives you the *authority* to write the piece and this is important. Whether you can include your story or not depends on the publication.

If you write about your own experience and add some useful information that can make a good article. But add the stories of a few other people who did the same thing and your piece becomes much richer.

There was a time when mainstream publications (the ones you see for sale in big newsagents) wanted their features to be objective. But now we have what I call 'the reality TV age' and things are changing. Some publications will now be happy to include details of your story. If in doubt, study the publication to see what its style is before you offer your own story.

Most true-life stories present a problem or conflict allowing readers to identify with the human responses even if they don't relate to the actual situation. The tone is usually positive, or at least has an upbeat ending, so even if something dreadful happened to you, good comes out of it, even if it is just that you learned something.

Writing about your experience forces you to shape your experiences until they can be fully understood by others.

Some magazines want to use your real name, others guarantee anonymity. Check first.

Writing about what and whom you know

If you have strong feelings about something or someone, then that could become an article. Think of the regular columnists you read in magazines. They tend to describe something that happened to them in great detail so you can empathise with them and 'be there' too. Your readers need to see, taste, touch, feel and hear just what you, the author, did.

To help you with this, think of topics such as divorce, being single, owning a pet, having visitors or holidaying with friends, and consider what you love and hate about these.

Use lots of anecdotes and be specific. Don't say how your divorce gave you freedom; describe it in terms that allow people to understand what freedom means to you and could mean for them, aspects they may not have thought of themselves. Perhaps you could say, for example, how your divorce allowed you to eat Pot Noodle from the tub for breakfast without feeling guilty.

Perhaps you could tell a story of something that happened to you. Paint a verbal picture, using the senses and emotion. This type of piece may describe a sequence of events in chronological order. Remember to give your story an upbeat ending, and use the conclusion to describe what you gained from the experience.

Writing a How To ...

This type of article is made up of facts. You need to convey to your readers why they should appreciate the process you describe. You could write about baking a cake, using the Internet or mending a flat tyre, but you could also describe how to communicate with your child or how to set up a writers' circle.

Think about what you know and ask yourself what skills you have that may not be shared by everyone else. Maybe you know how to leave your lover without him finding out, or how to settle your children overseas? Now think about who might be interested to know this too, and start looking for your market.

Sometimes a piece like this will benefit from a list of tips or steps that others will need to take in order to do the process you describe. Alliteration can be useful here, so if you can add a list such as Ten Tips for Finding Your Passion, Ten Tips for Riding a Bike in the Rain, Seven Secrets of Perfect Pastry or Six Steps to Publishing Success as this will add another dimension to this kind of article. A list will also provide the editor with the potential for putting your list in a box or frame and making a graphic out of it.

Where to find ideas

Read. The more you read, the more you will be inspired. Read newsletters, magazines, newspapers, and articles on the Internet. If you find an article that interests you consider how you could tackle the same idea for a different publication and how you might change it.

Listen. If you listen to what other people are talking about and what tend to be popular topics, you might just come up with an idea for a topical article.

Network. Keep making new friends and finding out about them. Be interested in other people. They will give you some great ideas.

Writers' Circles. Join or start one. They are a great source of friends as well as inspiration. Give 10 people the same topic to write about and they will all pick a different angle. Be inspired by the inspiration of others.

HOMEWORK ASSIGNMENT ONE

STEP ONE

Take a piece of paper and mark it out in six columns. At the top of each column write:

1. Who I am
2. What I know about
3. Where I have lived
4. Who I know
5. What I have done
6. What I am passionate about

If you want to do this on a computer, and submit your response to this step, then you could use the Table function in Word or create a chart in Excel. Alternatively you can print out the one I have created for you on the next page and fill it in by hand.

STEP TWO

Write for no less than five minutes, filling in every column of the chart until you can think of no more. Don't think about it too much. Write from your heart. The first things that come into your head will be fine. Try to complete the table by going across the columns from left to right, rather than filling it in one column at a time. This will stretch your brain nicely!

STEP THREE

Now consider all the things *you* could write about these facts. Give yourself at least 15 minutes to think about all the articles you could write based on what you have learned so far. For each article idea you have, write a short outline. You can take a look at my student, Adriana's, responses at the end of this lesson for inspiration.

Think about how you could turn that idea into an article that shares what you know.

If you get a bit stuck, then to help you get an angle on your topic, start each idea with the words 'How to'. For example, you may have written in the 'Who am I' column that you are a mother of teenagers. Your article idea could be:

How to parent teenagers
Or
How to speak to teenagers so they will listen
Or
How to talk to teenagers about the facts of life

Come up with as many 'How to' ideas as you can for each entry on your list.

STEP FOUR

Pick three of your favourite ideas from your long list.

SUBMIT three outlines of no more than 100 words each, one for each of the three topics. In each outline, I would like you to tell me:

1. What you will write about.
2. What makes this a fresh and exciting angle.
3. What kind of publication might find this interesting.

STEP FIVE

Create a new document in Word and use it to send your initial list, your list of ideas and then the three outlines.

Name your document with your name, DA (for *Definite Articles*) and the lesson number. So, if your name is Mary Smith you would name your file MarySmithDA1.

STEP SIX

Send this document to your personal tutor by email who will then mark it and send it back to you within two weeks.

Now you can start reading and working with Lesson Two. However, do not submit the homework for the next Lesson Two until you have received your critique for Lesson One.

Who I am	What I know about	Where I have lived	Who I know	What I have done	What I am passionate about

HOMEWORK SAMPLE ONE

The following homework was submitted by Adriana. It comes from an earlier version of the course when I did not include the column 'What I am passionate about', but it will still give you the general idea.

PART A

	Who I am	What I know about	Where I have lived	Who I know	What I have done
1	Adriana	Working for international organizations	Slovakia	Expats in Vienna	Gave birth in the Netherlands
2	Slovakian with no roots there	Living abroad	Austria	Expats in the Hague	Lived in foreign countries, even alone with small child(ren)
3	Expatriate	Giving birth and raising children abroad	Italy		Worked in many international organizations
4	Multicultural mother and wife	Past lives	Netherlands		Joined women's organizations
5	Person in quest for meaning of life	Women's organizations			Attended writing workshops in Voorschoten
6	Shopaholic	Travelling			Attended past-life regression workshop in Bergen
7	Interior designer wanna-be	Spiritual quest			Attended goddess within and dreams workshops in Amsterdam

PART B

My three top ideas:

1. Spiritual quest – for instance past life regression (workshop experience and overall knowledge)
2. Multicultural wife and mother
3. Expat and living abroad (struggles and opportunities)

PART C

My outlines:

Spiritual quest

This topic interests me deeply, and I believe it interests everyone else as well. We just keep ourselves busy and pre-occupied to the extent that we simply do not have the energy to face the basic existential dilemmas of our lives. In these articles I could write about the past life regression workshop I have attended, and perhaps even attend other things in order to be able to write about them. The publications interested in my quest would be those writing about topics that are spiritual, alternative, health and/or psychology related.

Multicultural wife and mother

This is a lighter topic and I would write about the daily struggles of being in a multicultural marriage and raising children in a multicultural environment. This would include the dilemma of languages such as the children's 'mother tongue', intercultural misunderstandings and advantages. I guess it would be written in a light and perhaps funny style, nothing too burdening or depressing. Publications that would be interested include expat newsletters and magazines, children's magazines, as well as publications of international schools, international societies and organizations.

Expat and living abroad

This topic would be in more of an informative style, informing and letting others know what it is like to live abroad, work abroad, have children abroad, and go through life in general abroad. How hard it can be just to have a cup of coffee without knowing the language or culture, not even speaking of getting insurance or finding a doctor. In this area, I would write about day-to-day mundane things, which can become quite difficult in an international setting. The type of publications interested would be again be expat newsletters and magazines, and publications of international groups, schools, associations and organizations.

LESSON TWO

Being a Writer

Morning Pages

Even the best writers suffer from writer's block sometimes. One of the best ways to fill yourself up with ideas is by writing a few pages longhand at the start of the day. It is important that you complete the exercise with a pen in hand as you need to access the right, creative, side of your brain, and using a computer tends to use the left, logical side. So buy yourself an attractive A5 lined notebook and a nice pen with which to work. My current notebook is bright orange in colour and has a ring binding. The ring binding makes it as easy to write on the left side of the page as the right, and lets the ideas continue to flow more easily. If you choose a journalist's notebook with a spiral at the top, you can write on one side of the paper only before flipping the book and continuing on the other sides. Choose the book that works best for you.

Try writing three pages of longhand every day. Mornings are best because that is when you remember your dreams. However, many of you will find it easier to write at some other time of day, and of course that's fine too. Halfway through the three pages you'll see the trivial writing disappear and your subconscious start to talk. Many established writers see these morning pages as their talisman.

Through morning pages you can learn about yourself. Write about the things that obsess you, worry you. Talk things through. The notebook is like a counsellor. It will not pass judgement.

Try not to take the pen off the paper, and keep on going. It's as if another force is driving the pen. Find the skeletons in the cupboard. Find out what makes you tick. Use the pages to find solutions.

Speedwriting

In her excellent workbook, *The Artist's Way*, Julia Cameron uses what she terms 'Morning Pages' as both therapy and a method of self-understanding. Natalie Goldberg, author of *Writing Down the Bones*, is another advocate of this kind of writing. She calls it 'Speedwriting'. Others may call this *free writing, stream of consciousness writing* or *flow*. A full-time writer, Goldberg uses the pages as a place to find ideas and slow her mind. She writes far more than three pages a day. Sometimes she goes to a café and writes all day long, bribing herself with cappuccinos and Oreo cookies along the way. Natalie reckons this is the only way to quiet her internal censor, which she calls 'Monkey Mind'. Like a monkey on your shoulder, it tells you that what you write is rubbish, selfish and useless. Keep the pen on the paper and keep writing. If your mind seems blank just write 'I don't know what to write'. As if by magic, after a page or two, that monkey will calm down, trust me!

Go out and be inspired

You cannot expect your morning pages to be filled with great insights and ideas if you do not allow yourself to think. Try to give yourself at least half an hour a week for thinking time. Take the time to switch off and let the ideas come. Take a bath, a walk, shop alone or sit down and listen to some classical music. You must be alone and not distracted by conversation for this to be effective.

One of the first things you discover when you take time out for inspiration is that you start to notice details – the way the light falls on a leaf, the way a blackbird scuffles in the dry beech leaves. You notice the silvery purple of the pigeon's breast and the way the mountains are a different colour every day.

Now you have lots to write about in your Morning Pages. And more still to put into your articles and stories.

Go outside, be alone and start paying attention to all that is around you. The sights, sounds, smells and tastes. Watch the world become tecnicolour. Taking this time to pay attention is what Julia Cameron calls an 'Artist's Date'. Visit a park, a lake, even go to a shopping mall or restaurant – and just observe, listen, think.

If you just sit at the table or computer and write write write, you never have time to go out and gain new experiences and your well of ideas will dry up. You may even become a creative anorexic.

Go to a café like Natalie Goldberg did and observe while you write. Make things up about people. Turn them into the characters in your stories. Fill that well.

While you are following this e-course try to write Morning Pages and take Artist's Dates as often as possible. This will keep the ideas flowing.

Dealing with blocks

There are always so many perfect excuses for not writing. You are too busy or too tired. Or maybe you feel it is a selfish exercise, because you're taking time just for you? But if you don't do it you will resent the other things that take your time instead.

Sometimes you tell yourself you are no good. That's only *an inner critic* that doesn't know what it is talking about. Don't pay it any attention. If you speedwrite, that 'monkey' will go away.

If you are blocked and speedwriting isn't working, go out for a while on the lookout for inspiration. That way you will feel as if you are being proactive rather than unproductive.

How to live a writer's life

If you are to have a writer's life you need to think and act like a writer. This may mean you will need to make a few changes. But mostly, it means that you will have to start carrying a notebook and pen around with you at all times and to stay on permanent alert for ideas. Here is a list of things that I recommend you start doing right away.

Twenty-five ways to live like a writer

1   Keep an ideas book.

2   Note resources as you find them: books with author, title, publisher; URLs of useful websites; organisations, with a description and URL

3   Jot down interesting facts, quotes and statistics that you see in other articles, on or offline.

4   Note quotes with source – who said it, when they said it, and where they said it.

5   When you have a great idea for an article, jot down a possible title and a few notes about what you would write about.

6   Keep business cards and brochures from people who could be useful to you some day. Write notes on the back of them saying when and where you met and what you talked about. If you don't you may forget.

7   Keep in touch with people. So, when you pick up that interesting business card, email the person and start to build a relationship. Save the email in your address book. Endeavour to stay in touch.

8   Ask your friends for connections to people you could interview and for the names of websites and publications you could write for.

9   A writer is only as good as her information sources/network – so be constantly hungry for new websites, people, ideas and organisations.

10 Start a blog. Make sure you stick to a theme that you could sustain, such as expat golfing, divorced single mother in Spain, Portuguese property developing and so on. Use this to practise working to deadlines and to increase your online presence. Later you will use it to link to all your published work.

11 Open a Twitter account. Use this to source ideas, connect with interesting people and to tell people about your published work and your blog. There's more on this in Lesson Seven.

12 Spot opportunities everywhere, all the time.

13 Ask for permission to quote people in whatever you publish.

14 Read existing publications and be inspired to write similar pieces yourself.

15 Speedwrite every day for 10 minutes or at the start of your working day.

16 Write a journal on holiday with quotes, sources and useful details such as names of tour companies, keep brochures.

17   Take notes every time you go to a talk, looking for quotes. Collect business cards from all the speakers you hear.

18   Keep records of your interviews for three years.

19   Have an Artist's Date once a week.

20   Pay attention.

21   Listen out for good quotes all the time.

22   Look out for patterns and metaphors in your experiences, like, for example, that building a business is like building a house and that you need to start with foundations. These insights can inspire your more personal articles and columns and particularly your blog.

23   Spot opportunities to group people together who have something in common and write about their specialism using them as case studies.

24   Look out for things that could become Ten Tips, Seven Steps, Six Secrets and so on.

25   Collect samples of magazines and books that you could write for or copy.

HOMEWORK ASSIGNMENT **TWO**

STEP ONE

Take at least one Artist's Date this week. Start paying attention.

Try speedwriting for yourself now or first thing in the morning. Make sure you have a quiet place to sit, and a pen and paper that you enjoy working with. Take the subject 'I love'. Set the timer and write for 10 minutes. If you can't get started then simply write 'I don't know what to write' or 'journeys' over and over again. Go wherever your thoughts take you.

STEP TWO

Speedwriting is a good way to generate potential ideas for articles. Take a moment to reread what you have written. What new ideas have emerged from your writing?

Write an outline of about 100 words for up to three ideas that could grow from your speedwriting.

In the outline you need to tell me:

1. What you will write about.

2. What makes this a fresh and exciting angle.

3. What kind of publication might find this interesting.

STEP THREE

Create a new document in Word and use it to submit your initial list, your list of ideas and then the three outlines.

Name your document with your name, DA (for *Definite Articles*) and the lesson number. So, if your name is Mary Smith you would name your file MarySmithDA2.

Send this document to your personal tutor by email who will then mark it and send it back to you within two weeks.

Now you can start reading and working with Lesson Three. However, do not submit the homework for the next Lesson Three until you have received your critique for Lesson Two.

HOMEWORK SAMPLE TWO

The following homework was submitted by Renata, who is from South Africa and has lived in Italy and Holland.

PART B

1) 'Married and divorced by 30' (psyche piece)

What I'd write about: I'd interview three or four women/men who have been divorced by 30. I'd also interview a psychologist, relationship therapist, divorce lawyer and possibly a mediator. I'd look into why the marriages broke down, if this is a trend, what the parties involved have learnt, what effect the divorce has had on them... I'd also include tips on how to approach the situation regarding practical aspects like dividing assets and responsibilities towards kids (if applicable).

What makes this a fresh and exciting angle: Divorce is often dealt with in women's magazines, but generally for an older target market. General trends for the past two decades suggested women were getting married later (I'd have to substantiate this), yet here we have people marrying young, but divorcing young too. It'd be interesting to know what sort of things are causing divorce at such a young age, as well as the practicalities of divorce in your 20s.

What kind of publication might find this interesting: Any women's magazine (South Africa/UK): *Fairlady* (SA), *Destiny* (SA), *Cosmo, Marie Claire, Women and Home*, Essentials, *Elle, Reality Magazine* (SA), *Psychologies...*

2) 'Studying in Italy'

What I'd write about: How it felt to study in an Umbrian hilltop town, surrounded by medieval city walls and sites dating back to 4 BC. I'd go into the more practical aspects (finding accommodation, dealing with culture shock, living expenses, the unbearable heat and mosquitoes in summer, the rail system and getting to other Italian cities, the 'drink and snog' nightlife etc) I'd include sidebars on:
   a) How to make the most of your experience (like: try not to hang out only with people from your own country; refuse to speak your mother tongue for the duration of your stay; etc)
   b) Top 10 must-sees in Perugia/Umbria

What makes this a fresh and exciting angle: An *honest* firsthand account of studying in Perugia.

What kind of publication might find this interesting: *Transitions Abroad: Language Study Abroad* (preferably aimed at one of their writer's competitions)

3) 'Adventures in a 50m radius'

What I'd write about: I'd write about the advantages of exploring your own neighbourhood – cheap 'travel', getting to know your community (important for expats), feeling you belong (important for expats), finding real local gems (whether new shops or experiences), increasing your creativity by really engaging with your environment, exercise. I'd start with my own neighbourhood – walking in Morstraat in Leiden, I'd start on my challenge to find at least 15 fascinating things within a 50m radius of my front door.

What makes this a fresh and exciting angle: This is travel and exploration, as well as a bit of 'What's on'/'What to do', in an unusual guise. It's a great way to write about traveling on a budget, as all you have to do is step out your own door, *and* you (and the reader) get to know your own neighbourhood too.

What kind of publication might find this interesting: This could be a great regular piece for any national newspaper or hyperlocal publications like HagueOnline and Expatica (or I could pitch it to a travel magazine as a regular column that would be based in different cities in the Netherlands.) It could even be a regular piece for *Access:* The magazine could challenge readers (or freelance writers) to explore within a 10m radius of their own town/cities/homes.

LESSON THREE

How to Write What Editors Want

Keeping the market in mind

Whatever you write, you must have the market in mind. Always. Before you send off a story you have to research your market. You need to study not just the articles themselves to see what type of material they are publishing, but also the advertising, the readers' letters and advertorials. A magazine will often favour pieces that tie in nicely with their regular advertisers. So, if they have lots of estate agents' advertisements, articles on buying houses or moving will go down well.

Obtain three recent back issues of a magazine you would like to write for and study it in detail. Many magazines are now available online so you will be able to view back issues on the Internet. Magazines such as *Living Abroad* at www.livingabroadmagazine.co.uk put a selection of articles on their website. And that is a good place to start. If you want to see a complete issue you could try *Away* magazine from Brussels at www.awaymagazine.be.

If you can't find the articles online then write or email the publication's media department and ask to buy the copies. Sometimes they will be happy to send them to you for free anyway.

Take a look at the magazines and study the contents page to see which kinds of features they use in every issue. These topics often also appear in the magazine along the top of the page too, like a header. Lifestyle, beauty, family, travel and so on. If they have regular sections then it is a good idea to pitch articles that will fit them perfectly in length, style and tone.

What to look for in a magazine

Study magazines in detail in order to work out exactly what kind of pieces they are likely to buy from you.

Look at the contents list, cover lines (that's the teaser text they use on the cover to tempt you to buy the magazine), the type of models they use, the types of article and their average word count. Notice too who writes their letters and who would be attracted to the advertisements. This gives you a great clue as to the publication's typical readers.

Notice the length of a typical sentence, paragraph and article. Do they use long words or short ones? How many sentences are in a paragraph? If the magazine is designed with three columns on a page, then a short paragraph can look quite long. Do they include a separate 'leader' paragraph between the title and the first paragraph? Do they include lots of information at the end? See that your copy mimics this.

Look to see whether the articles contain bullet points and lists, boxes of information, sidebars, out-take quotes or lots of subheadings. Make sure yours does the same.

On the following page you will find a chart that you could copy and complete to help you to analyse a magazine. It can be surprisingly revealing and I recommend you complete this exercise for the first few publications to which you are serious about pitching.

Article analysis chart

Sections	Article lengths	Typical features
Home truths	800 words	Lots of photos First person Extensive sidebars
Healthy living	600 – 1200 words	Product images Reviews One personal health survival story

Contributor's guidelines

Most publications put their submission criteria on their websites. So look out for their *contributors'* or *writers' guidelines* and rates of pay, print them out and study them carefully. Often these will give you great clues as to what the publication is really looking for.

Contributors' guidelines usually include the following:

- types of piece
- length of piece
- style of piece
- illustrations and how to supply them – print or JPEG, and the size and dpi (resolution)
- hard copy or email attachment; pdf or formatted document
- rates of pay
- payment terms
- time lapse before publication
- syndication rights
- copyright details

Here are the writers' guidelines for *Woman Abroad*

I was editor of this magazine for two years and, while it is sadly no longer around, this will give you a good idea of the kind of things all editors want. Read them carefully.

WRITERS' GUIDELINES
WOMAN ABROAD

The magazine written and read by women on the move (mostly!)

Writers' Guidelines

Readers

Woman Abroad is aimed at today's mobile woman. She may be resident abroad as an expatriate or an expatriate spouse, or simply be living and working in mobile communities. The magazine is designed to inform, entertain, inspire and support women abroad and their families. It is also noted for building a sense of community among its readers. Its international readers, aged from 25-55, speak English fluently yet this may not be their first language.

Readers are interested in all aspects of life on the move, including profiles of famous/reputable expatriates, third culture children, conferences, language, marriage, education, property, hobbies, portable careers, expatriate employment, humour, virtual business, books, arts, travel, self-development, health, gardening, sport, home, finance and relocation issues. First-person pieces include 'View from here' (what it is really like to live in X) and 'In my own words', a piece about a dramatic real-life experience. We are keen to receive case studies (with career path) of successful women who have developed a portable career.

Style and content

Most articles are written in the third person, although a diary style may be appropriate in some cases. Where possible articles should contain quotations from a range of expatriates and/or professional bodies/experts. A short piece (700 words) must focus on just one or two aspects of the issue. Any longer pieces (interviews or features up to 1500 words) should be in depth, offering insight into emotions, cultural adaptation and challenges in addition to the facts. Sidebars giving information about associated books, magazines, websites or organisations should be included with at least a URL or contact number. Content must be politically correct and non-discriminatory. There is no need to hide the objective truth.

The style is upbeat, friendly, clear and concise, without too many polysyllabic words. The reader is addressed in the second person. Sentences and paragraphs are generally short. Single quotes are used, not double. Dialogue begins a new line and is indented. The first time a person is quoted their full name will be used; after that surname or first name only. Paragraphs are indented without line spaces between. Numbers to nine are in words, above

10 are in figures. Full stops (periods) are not used after Mr, Mrs, in acronyms and so on. Abbreviations such as etc, ie, eg and nb are avoided. Spelling is British.

Suggested titles and subheadings should be provided. A passport style photograph of the writer may be requested and should be submitted by email in PDF/EDS format where possible. Potential illustrations may be suggested.

Where possible, writers should have firsthand experience of life overseas so that they can empathise with the readers.

IMPORTANT
- Spelling is British NOT American.
- Please use single NOT double quotation marks.
- Please try NOT to write over the commissioned length or you may be penalised.

Writing to Length
It is very important to us that you write the length specified at the time you are commissioned. We can only fit about 800 words maximum on a single page; if we are to have a photograph, 700-750 words is perfect. Please write to length unless we agree, after discussion, to allocate more space.

Please ensure that the body of your text keeps to the word length. Sidebars can eat into extra words, but may well be cut. If you feel unable to write the body text to the required length you may find your fee has been reduced according to the time it has taken for us to cut it for you. Features are usually 1200, 1500 or 2000 words only. We always like to include a bio of the writer on the page. These words should not be included in the word count.

Author bios
Please provide us with a little bit about you – a short biography to go with your piece, preferably with a contact email or website. This must not exceed 40 words.

Deadlines
Once a piece has been commissioned, it must be submitted by email at least two months prior to its proposed publication date.

Illustrations
If you are able to provide appropriate illustrations for your article, we will sometimes pay upwards of £25 for a small photograph. Photographs need to be copyright free or copyright of the author and of good quality for reproduction. Transparencies or prints approximately 17cms x 12cms or a digital image are preferred. Digital images must be properly scanned and

supplied 300 dpi to the reproduction size – normally A5 (28cms x 20cms) – and a JPEG image is preferred.

However, we will only consider paying for photographs taken specifically for the article. All payment is at the discretion of the designer. No submissions to 'In my own words' will be considered without good quality photographs of the writer. It is always appreciated if you can give ideas and sources for illustrations.

Woman Abroad gives you wings
We are committed to supporting expatriates in every way we can:

If you are a relatively new writer
Of course, we would like you to have a portfolio stuffed with clippings, but this is not imperative. All you need is a passion for your topic and an accessible writing style. Woman Abroad kick-starts the careers of budding expatriate writers and endeavours to publish new writers alongside established journalists. New writers requiring more sub-editing than normal may receive a reduced fee of no less than 50 per cent of the standard rate. This is at the discretion of the editor and her decision is final.

Submitting your ideas
Email the editor, Joanna Parfitt (ed@womanabroad.com), in the first instance outlining your ideas. Each idea should comprise: suggested title; one sentence synopsis of the content; an idea of the kind of people you would to speak to for quotations; clear indication of the objective of the piece. A sample of about 500 words of your writing style (preferably published) should be included along with reference to any previous publications (if possible).

What we would like to know
New ideas are welcomed. Letters on all aspects of the magazine or expatriate life will be considered for publication in Woman Abroad or on its accompanying website. If you would like to tell us about interesting success stories, your own success, or any Internet sites, products, services or events other expatriates might like to know about, please get in touch. Our problem page welcomes letters too, and can help with personal, professional, physical or other areas. If you have a story, but really feel unable to write about it yourself then we can find you a writer to work with.

Rights
Although the magazine will be read worldwide we ask to purchase First British Serial Rights on any pieces. Second Rights are occasionally purchased and a lower fee effected.

Any article purchased by us may also appear on the Woman Abroad website (www.womanabroad.com) but no additional fee will be paid.

Payment

Most pieces are no more than 750 words in length, though some features may stretch to 1200, 1500 or 2000 words. Payment starts at £100 for a piece. Experienced journalists will be paid £200 per 1000 words, though fiction (1000-1500 words) earns no more than £150. Any commissioned illustrations will be paid for at a previously agreed rate. Payment is made straight after publication of your piece, when a copy of the magazine will be mailed with your cheque.

Lead time
Some articles have been commissioned up to six issues ahead. Please be prepared to be patient if we are to use your work.

If you want to study more guidelines like this then *enRoute* magazine has some particularly good ones. Find them at:

http://enroute.aircanada.com/en/articles/writers-guidelines

The website *Freelance Writing* has a huge database of writers' guidelines at:

http://www.freelancewriting.com/guidelines/pages/index.php

The Eight As for Astounding Articles

There are eight things that will make an editor prick up her ears and seriously consider your idea whether you've had anything published before or not.

Each of these secrets begins with the letter A, so that should make it easier for you to remember. Eight 'A's.

1) Authority

The first one is authority.

Authority means that you need to be able to convince the editor that you know about your subject. Sometimes acting in a confident manner is as much as you need. If you want to write about Milan, you could have authority about the place because you've been to Milan on holiday for ten years, or because you've had a Milanese boyfriend/girlfriend or because you have lived there. If you want to write about psychology you may have worked in the mental health field, interviewed several psychiatrists, or perhaps you've lived with somebody who has been mentally ill. Experience and authority doesn't have to derive from the fact that you are a world expert, have written a book on the subject, or have been there and done that for decades. Show that you're an authority on the subject by being able to prove why you know a lot about it.

2) Accessibility

The second 'A' is accessibility.

It is important that you write in a simple style, using short sentences and short paragraphs. The best thing to do is to look at the sort of articles that are in your target magazine before you submit anything. Count how many words are in a sentence, how many words are in a paragraph and how many words are in an article. Then you'll know what that magazine will want.

Remember that articles are usually designed into two or three columns. This means that the paragraphs are going to be very narrow. In this case a paragraph that is made of just two 16-word sentences could look like a rather dense paragraph once it is in a column. Take a look at a magazine or paper until you find a paragraph that runs the whole length of a column. It can look boring, even if it isn't. That's why you have to count the paragraphs and the sentences to see how the professionals do it. It's also good to notice details, such as whether the articles have lots of subheadings in bold or a larger type, indicating each slight change of topic. Look carefully at the sections and, again, count the words, the number of sentences and the number of paragraphs. You'd be surprised by how many paragraphs are only one sentence long. If you want to write in an accessible way then you need to do some research like this before you start.

You can make an article easy to read by making sure there's lots of white space on the paper, by using short words and short sentences. There's no point using long, clever words that have the reader dashing for the dictionary, it doesn't impress anyone. A magazine is targeted at a specific type of reader and no editor will want to alienate her precious subscribers or readers by acting too clever. Long words can make the reader feel inferior, and you do not want that. So, as a rule, you need to use words that somebody for whom English is not a first language would be able to understand. Think of writing for a 13 year old and you should get the level right.

If you do use foreign words, make sure that you make their meaning clear to the reader. So, put the foreign word in italic and ensure you explain it's meaning too.

3) Authenticity

The third 'A' is authenticity.

A bit of an odd one, maybe? But you see it is very difficult to write something if you don't really understand it or you don't really believe in it. If I wanted to write an article about coffee, let's say, and I didn't drink coffee, it would be pretty difficult to conjure up the kind of passion that I would need to make somebody want to buy some coffee beans or go out and buy a cup of special cappuccino. It really helps if you believe in your subject. Now, if I had to do a piece about coffee and hated drinking it myself, I could get round this by being authentic, by being honest. I could start the article by saying 'I hate the smell of coffee first thing in the morning' or something about the increase in outlets selling take away coffee. Or how difficult it is to drink out of those polystyrene cups with plastic lids and how you watch coffee dribbling down commuters' chins on the morning train? If you need to write about finding a good cup of coffee yet do not drink it, you might like to talk to people who do have opinions. To be authentic you need to believe in what you're writing, even if you do not believe in the product itself. If you go to see and review a new play at the theatre and you don't really like it, then you need to say so. It can be tough being honest.

4) Authorship

And our fourth 'A' is authorship.

Authorship is all about behaving like a professional writer. If your target magazine has articles that are 700 words long, you submit articles that are 700 words long. If you write 1500 they are likely to reject the article, even if you produced a great piece. You see they've got to pay somebody to cut half of your article out again and they may have neither the time nor the money to do this. If you are lucky, they may return the piece to you and ask you to cut it yourself, but they will be wary of using you again in the future. If the magazine wants you to write it by the 4th Dec, say, you write it by the 4th Dec. If the magazine says 'please use single quotation marks not double', you use single quotation marks. If they want British spelling, you use British spelling. That's what being an author is all about — getting it right and working according to the writers' guidelines. Most magazines will provide you with writers' guidelines so that you know what they want. They may provide them on a website or can send them to you as an email attachment. These guidelines will tell you the kind of style and tone they want, whether they want subheadings or not and the kind of language they require, whether they want lots of dialogue or quotations or statistics.

5) Attention

The fifth 'A' stands for attention.

If you don't catch the attention of the editor in the first sentence of your cover letter you don't stand a chance. The first paragraph of your article is the most important of all, it needs to catch the attention of the reader and hang onto it so that he or she keeps reading. It needs to catch the attention of the editor so that he or she[†] will want to commission you again. The title you choose for the piece needs to be compelling too. And you need to write a great leader.

6) Appropriate

The sixth 'A' is for appropriate.

It is vital that your article is appropriate for the publication and its readers. That it is pitched at the right level and with information that is relevant, timely and interesting. There is no point pitching an article on train spotting for retired people to a parenting magazine, or pitching a short story to a magazine that never has them.

7) Alchemy

The seventh 'A' is my favourite. It stands for Alchemy.

Alchemy is the art of making gold, seemingly out of secret ingredients. It is about magic and wow factors. Good journalists are never short on ideas, they see the potential for stories everywhere they go. They network and read and go to conferences so that they can be constantly on the look out for new ideas, new experts, new sources. Try to put a bit of magic into your articles.

8) Added value

And now for the eighth 'A', an 'A' that can make all the difference. Added Value.

If you can provide more than just an article that really helps. Maybe you can offer a free gift or a discount? Or you can include a resource box, or sidebar, with a list of further reading or useful websites. If you provide extra information like this, the article

---

† Please note that for purposes of consistency from now on I will be using 'she' or 'her' whenever 'he or she' or 'his or her' could be written.

becomes more useful and the reader is likely to keep it for future reference. Editors love that.

So, to recap, you need to prove that you know what you're talking about, that's *authority*, show that you care about it, that's *authenticity*, write in a simple style that's right for the magazine, that's accessibility, then write and submit it in the way the magazine wants, which is *authorship*. Do your best to grab the *attention* of the editor and the reader, take care to submit things that are *appropriate* and don't forget to be an *alchemist* and add a touch of magic. Finally, *add some more value* by thinking about what you could put in a resources box at the end.

HOMEWORK ASSIGNMENT THREE

Now that you have learned about contributor's guidelines and how to hone your ideas, you need to put this into practise.

STEP ONE

Find two magazines (on or offline) that you would like to write for and get hold of their writers'/contributor's guidelines. Read the guidelines and study the magazines carefully. You can complete the chart I gave you earlier in this lesson if you like.

STEP TWO

Based on what you have learned please write me outlines of one possible article that you could write for each of those two publications. Create a possible title for each piece, and say where it would fit in the magazine (in the Lifestyle or Travel section, for example). Outline the piece in one or two paragraphs.

STEP THREE

Create a new document in Word and use it to submit your assignment.

Name your document with your name, DA (for *Definite Articles*) and the lesson number. So, if your name is Mary Smith you would name your file MarySmithDA3.

Send this document to your personal tutor by email who will then mark it and send it back to you within two weeks.

Now you can start reading and working with Lesson Four. However, do not submit the homework for the next Lesson Four until you have received your critique for Lesson Three.

HOMEWORK SAMPLE THREE

Violetta submitted the following homework.

MAGAZINE #1: *Fairlady* (a South African general-interest women's magazine)

Working title:

'The Future of the Book...'

Section:

Talking point (features topical articles; often the 'harder' stories in an issue)

Outline:

Introductory thoughts: People are quick to either defend or dismiss the future role of the printed book, or codex. We've already seen the demise of many print newspapers [some examples here] and a general movement towards online content and advertising. Technological developments, such as e-readers and tablets (the *iPad*, as well as Blackberry's recent *PlayBook*) appear to threaten the printed form. Where do we stand and what do we have to lose... or gain?

Examining the arguments 'for' and 'against' the book: This will briefly mention some of the research and opinions of international scholars such as Robert Darnton, Jason Epstein, Kevin Kelly and Jeff Gomez. I'd also speak to three local publishers about their strategies regarding traditional and online-based publishing.

Points to ponder: Barring the final printing, books already are digital; the beauty of print-on-demand (Espresso Book Machines); the paradox of technology – the better it gets and the quicker it changes and the more we have to update our reading devices; examining our 'love' for the book...

Sidebar: 'Reverse publishing' – examples of authors and bloggers who have gone from online to print, *against* the online trend, and why?

MAGAZINE #2: *easyJet Traveller*

Working title:

'Greenest Holland'

Section:

Main feature (there are usually two or three per issue)

Outline:

Focus: Though most tourists head to Amsterdam, The Hague or Maastricht, the country's natural reserves, at first glance unassuming, are surprisingly expansive and varied. And while there 'ain't no mountain high enough for serious hiking, there are plenty of cool, green, crowd-free sanctuaries to escape to...

The top 5 green spots:

1. Utrechtse Heuvelrug (province of Utrecht): description; highlights; hidden gem; how to get there; contact details.

2. Nationaal Park Weerribben-Wieden (Overijssel): description; highlights; hidden gem; how to get there; contact details.

3. De Hoge Veluwe (Gelderland): description; highlights; hidden gem; how to get there; contact details.

4. Maasduinen Nationaal Park (Limburg): description; highlights; hidden gem; how to get there.

5. Zuid-Kennemerland (Noord-Holland): description; highlights; hidden gem; how to get there; contact details.

Sidebar:

Where to stay in each nature reserve/area (low- to high-budget accommodation).

LESSON FOUR

Writing an effective article

Crafting an article is a lot of work, so this topic has been stretched over two lessons.

What makes an article?

An article must be interesting or entertaining enough for someone to want to read it. In other words, it must have a point, or a purpose. The reader should feel different, think differently or feel they have benefited in some way from reading it. In general an article should fulfil one or more of the criteria, below.

An article must do one or more of the following:

- Inspire
- Inform
- Support
- Entertain

It should teach something, shed insight on an issue, and support the reader by sharing stories of people with whom they can empathise. It could make them laugh, make them cry or just make them feel better. If you fulfil one of these criteria then your article will have purpose.

Ten types of article

Here are ten ideas for what I consider to be the most popular types of article you could write and place:

1. Features – often written in the third person and with quotes and information and case studies on a theme, often has subheads and sidebars

2. How to articles – how to make dinner for a tenner

3. Tips – ten ways to improve your golf swing

4. Interviews with one person

5. Interviews with several people all on the same theme

6. Reviews – book, play, event, music, product, restaurant

7. Travel – usually has subheads and lists of extra information, known as 'sidebars'

8. Letters to the editor

9. Columns – always personal and insightful, sometimes humorous

10. Journalistic – an objective round up of information, or report on a given topic, such as 'what is blogging', or, 'understanding Alzheimer's'

How to craft a features article

Although there are many optional 'ingredients' you could use in your articles, the following are the most important:

- Title
- Leader
- Beginning
- Middle
- End
- Sidebars
- Author bio
- Illustrations (optional)

Let me explain each in more detail:

Title

Try to provide a snappy headline/title. Make sure it is compelling. Maybe it alliterates, includes a pun or answers a good question.

Leader

Write your own leader/standfirst/sell/slug – that's a sentence that comes after the headline and gives a short description of the aim of the piece. It will usually include your name too. If you cannot summarise the purpose of your article in a sentence or so, then your content is not focused enough. It is common to do the leader in italics.

> *Jane Dalton talks to three interior designers and discovers that clearing clutter is a messy business.*

Beginning

It must have a beginning that arrests the reader and makes them want to continue – this will set the scene for the main body of the piece (middle). It will usually last one or two paragraphs and be no more than 25 per cent of the text. I think that less than 20 per cent is better. (Beginnings are covered in more detail in Lesson Five.)

Middle

It must have a middle that fulfils the promise of the title and leader. This is the largest portion of the article and it may comprise facts, quotations, case studies and anecdotes. It will usually be fast paced and absorbing. It must be informative.

- **Rule of three:** Whatever you put in the middle of a features article, I always try to use the *rule of three* – let me explain. If you plan to feature something, such as ideal caravan sites, you should mention at least three different ones. If you plan to feature a personal issue, such as divorce, I'd recommend that you speak to at least three different people who have that experience.

- **Dialogue:** Dialogue will make your piece come alive. The eye likes to see small chunks of text. Most articles are eventually laid out into two or three columns, so be aware that your paragraph lengths will look different accordingly. Add quotes from experts or case studies.

- **Facts:** Add some facts, statistics or valuable information that endorses your argument. Whenever you add statistics or facts you will need to quote the source. Maybe you read it in a newspaper, survey or heard someone say it at a conference. If so, you need to mention the source and date. (Middles are covered in more detail in Lesson Five.)

Ends

It must have a conclusion that fits in with the rest of the text and offers an appropriate ending. Maybe it will round up the facts or posit an insight that the middle text revealed. Sometimes it will be a call to action. Try not to make your conclusion more than 20 per cent of the whole of the article. (Ends are covered in more detail in Lesson Five.)

Sidebars

This is the term given to a list or box of extra information, such as useful contact addresses, websites, books, graphs or facts that comes at the end of the article. If your target publication uses them, then so must you. Sidebars add interest to a piece and can be used as illustration.

Illustrations

If associated photographs or graphics could be provided or suggested by you then say so. If you wrote about an artist, for example, then the publication will likely want a photograph of her in action. If you can supply one then this is a great benefit. Often the people you interview can supply their own quality images. If the magazine does not have a budget for images then you will be well received if you can fulfil this need.

Interviewing people

If you want to write features articles then the chances are that you will want to write about people and their own experiences as they pertain to your piece. For example, if you are writing about how a someone may feel when she is made redundant it would be a good idea to talk to three or more different people about their experiences. Unless you are writing for a men's or women's magazine, I would make sure that you interview a mixture of men and women and people of different ages and lifestyles. This will provide you with a balanced view.

However, there are a few things you need to know in order to be able to interview effectively so that you do not spend too much time and end up with just a handful of really useful quotes to use.

How to conduct an effective interview

Before you start the interview you need to do a bit of preparation. If not, then you may find you spend an hour in conversation, during which your interviewee talks about issues that do not relate to the article and you end up having taken far too much time with them.

When you write about someone you should:

- Ask the right questions
- Know the market
- Know the publication's objectives
- Know the reader
- Focus on as narrow a topic as you can
- Use the right ingredients
- Use the right recipe

Asking questions and interviewing

Ask questions that lead the interviewee towards the answer you want, if necessary.

Avoid closed questions – ones that result in a 'yes' or 'no' answer. What you want is full, clear, sentences.

The live interview

You talk at about 150 words a minute, and so when you interview someone for an article or profile you may only have space for 300 of their words (that is a third of the space on one page of a magazine). So you can't ask very many questions if you don't have much space.

If you do conduct your interviews, live or over the phone, then you need to be on the alert for the perfect quotes and insightful sentences that fall from your interviewee's lips fully formed. When you do a live interview, start off by making a few notes about the location, setting, date and so on. You may find that it will be appropriate to describe your interviewee in some way, the clothes she wears, her mannerisms and so on, so note these too.

Each time you hear a really great quote, write it down, verbatim, enclosing it in inverted commas so that when you go back to it later you know it was a real quote and not something you paraphrased.

Incidentally, when you do quote people you are able to paraphrase slightly so long as you retain the sense of what they are saying and the exact meaning. People stumble over words, stutter and repeat themselves. You are at liberty to tidy this up.
It can be most efficient to conduct interviews by email. Firstly, your interviewee has time to reflect and can reply at her own convenience, and secondly, you will have a record of their responses and do not need to transcribe an interview.

Interviewing Melody Biringer

Below is the first page of notes taken by me when Melody came to speak at the Women's Business Institute in The Hague. It provides a good example of Quote Spotting in action.

Melody Biringer, of The Crave Company (www.thecravecompany.com) at Women's Business Initiative (www.womensbusinessinitiative.net), The Hague, September 23rd 2010.

300 at launch of Crave book in Amsterdam yet a year ago knew one person here.

" All because of Twitter."

" I am a start-up junkie."

" I grew up on a strawberry farm and began picking strawberries when I was eight. It was the worst job in the world so the next day I started a lemonade stand. A week later I hired my cousins to run it."

Began Berry Barns - had 8 pick your own roadside shops by age of 18

Next - wicker furniture store. But wanted to live in the city: " on the top floor and be a multibillion-trillionaire."

Went to Seattle city

" I'd rather people saw what needed to be done and then do it than wait to be told what to do."

Had retail and wholesale business and 70 employees

" We go through life so busy we don't see our girlfriends."

" All my businesses have morphed or been sold or failed."

Started home spa parties, didn't go well, so had a big party for her network and called it Crave Party. Everything a woman craves. First party was a pyjama party and got lots of press.

" If something hits a nerve right away you need to pay attention to that."

But then wanted a business opportunity that was no leases, no employees and let her work on her laptop from anywhere — first stop Amsterdam.

Top tip: " Fail fast and get it out of your system."

The article that resulted and appeared on the Expatica website is below:

Inspiration from a Start-Up Junkie

Jo Parfitt tells the remarkable story of Melody Biringer, an inspirational woman who is a writer, entrepreneur and opportunist always seeking the next accomplishment.

September was a good month for the Netherlands, for this was the month that American self-styled Start-Up Junkie, Melody Biringer, sped into town, launched her gazillionth book and her twenty something business and zoomed on out again, leaving the lowlands scattered with some rather beautiful orange and pink books.

If you have missed the launch of *Crave Amsterdam* and you call yourself a female entrepreneur, then you must have been either out of town or asleep to miss the whirlwind that is Melody Biringer.

It was less than a year ago, at the I am Not a Tourist fair in Amsterdam, that I first met Biringer. She rather modestly showed me a battered copy of a fat orange paperback book, with the words *Crave Seattle* on the front, and told me just a little about the Crave events, parties and books that she was busy launching all over the US, and was just kind of wondering about bringing to Amsterdam.

Subtitling the guide 'The Urban Girl's Manifesto', the book is a showcase of some of the most remarkable women in town. Created in collaboration with a range of multi-cultural, multi-talented urban girls, it's a beautifully illustrated directory of female-owned businesses, among them some of the most innovative and creative talents around.

And then, last month, *Crave Amsterdam* was indeed launched and 300 people attended the event. A week later Biringer was in the Hague to speak to the members of the Women's Business Initiative, an innovative business led by another creative American woman – Suzy Ogé. The room was buzzing as we all waited to hear what this woman who acquires more businesses than handbags had to say.

"A year ago I knew one person," began Biringer, "and now look!" she raised her arms expansively. "And it's all because of Twitter." Thousands of people now know this publishing powerhouse and respect her for her dynamism and her ability to take an idea and run with it. Yet, after hearing her story, we respected her for her honesty, humility and authenticity too.

Biringer grew up in the country on a strawberry farm. As a child, she began picking fruit but soon tired of such back-breaking work and decided that what the workers needed was refreshment. Even at the young age of eight she had an eye for a business and proved herself to be amazingly savvy.

"So I started a lemonade stand," she paused. "And then a week later I persuaded my cousins to run it for me!"

From the lemonade stand she moved on as an 18-year-old to start eight pick-your-own roadside Berry Barns, still popular today. Then it was a wicker furniture store and that too was very successful.

"But I wanted to live in a city, on a top floor. I wanted to be a multi-billion-trillionaire. So I went to Seattle." There she started a retail and wholesale business that employed more than 70 people. It was successful, of course, but Biringer was not happy. She did not like managing people. "I'd rather people saw what needed to be done and then do it than wait to be told what to do," she said.

So that business ended and Biringer decided she wanted to be in the fitness game. Only she realised too late and after investing lots of money that she had picked the wrong location. This was one of the 20 or so businesses she has chalked up so far. Biringer is the first to admit that much of her initially brilliant ideas change into something completely different after a few months.

"They have all morphed or been sold or failed," she explained. But while busy starting businesses, she realised she was working too hard and had no time to see her girlfriends. Then she discovered that many of her girlfriends felt exactly the same way. And this was when she hit on the idea of the spa party, and the Crave Party was born. The concept was that these lavish events, complete with food, drink and spa treatments for all, provided everything a woman craved.

The email interview

Sometimes an email interview is the best option. Not only will you have a written record of what they really said, but your interviewee will also have more time to reflect on her answers and reply at their leisure.

If you are writing a piece of say, 700 words, you are unlikely to have room for more than nine quotes. And, if you are interviewing three people, as discussed earlier in the Rule of Three, that means three sentences or thereabouts per person. To achieve this you will need to ask just three questions.

When you conduct email interviews let your interviewee know that you want their answers to be in full sentences, and that you only need a maximum of 50 words per answer, for example. Tell them that their answers will be quoted verbatim or paraphrased. This will prepare them for your final piece.

In July 2010 I was interviewed by an online publication called Expat Arrivals. To illustrate the importance of the interview and to show how an email interview became a full-length feature, please take a look at the 'journey of an article', below.

The journey of an article – from email interview to finished piece

Watch how my interview with Stephanie Katz of www.expatarrivals.com became a full-length feature.

Stephanie contacted me with this message:

I'm the editor of www.expatarrivals.com, a site devoted to the development of comprehensive destination guides aimed at easing expats' transition abroad. Currently, I'm writing a feature on 'trailing spouses' and would very much like to interview you regarding your experiences. If interested please contact me directly at stephanie@expatarrivals.com. I look forward to hearing from you.

Best,
Stephanie

And these were her questions:

First off, Expat Arrivals is a fledgling website (not even one year old) that aims to be the ultimate guide for English-speaking expats moving overseas. We pride ourselves on objective and up-to-date information that prospective expats will find valuable prior, during and even after they've made their move. Currently we have guides addressing 65 destinations, and the site now attracts around 10,000 unique users each month/50,000 page views.

As mentioned, the feature I'm writing will address the trials and tribulations of 'trailing spouses', specifically addressing those expats moving to Middle Eastern countries.

Based on your blog it seems that in the beginning you had a quite a time of it; in this vein I'd like to write a piece that prepares spouses as best as possible and offers them a knowledge base that can make access easier.

Please feel free to answer as few or as many questions as you deem fit:

Q: What preparations did you make prior to your move? How much did you know about Dubai?

Q: How did your perceptions change upon arrival?

Q: What was most frustrating about your transition and why?

Q: What freedoms did you find the most difficult to do without?

Q: What outlets did you find worked best to remedy your frustration?

Q: What kept you from being able to work upon your arrival? In retrospect, what advice would you give to women that would like to work to avoid this hang-up?

Q: What resources did you use to solve your problem of employment once you were there?

Q: What resources did you use to build your social network? How important was building a social network to your **well-being**?

Q: What is the one best overall tip/piece of advice **you** could give to a spouse joining a husband who's been offered an overseas contract?

Q: What is the one logistical 'must do' that you could advise?

Q: How did the move **affect** you personal identity? How did it affect your ability to play a certain role and form relationships?

Q: How did the move **affect** the relationship between yourself and your husband? What problems did you encounter? How did you solve them?

If you feel I've left anything out, or if **there is** any additional information you'd like to include, **please say it** – it **would be** greatly appreciated. Personal anecdotes are always fantastic as well!

And here come my replies:

Q: What preparations did you make prior to your move? How much did you know about Dubai?

I actually moved there in 1987, the day after marrying Ian, who had been there for two years already. I had had two trips there to visit him before that and so knew a bit about what to expect. I would always recommend a recce trip. I was naïve, and made no other preparations and had no real expectations, high or low. Today, I would always recommend talking to people who are already there, reading guides, like the *Culture Smart!* guides, and connecting with those in the know. The website *Dubaiwoman* is very useful, but there are lots of others like that. Before my first trip though, pre-Internet, all I had done was find Dubai on a map. Today, I would use *Google Earth* and the many online forums to be really sure. The *Real Post Reports* at www.talesmag.com are pretty honest too. Since then, I have moved five times and been back to the Middle East on countless occassions – it has my heart, although it has changed immeasurably.

Q: How did your perceptions change upon arrival?

Being alone, with no company support meant that I became very isolated very quickly. My new husband was at work and I had no clue what to do or what I could do. I moved rapidly from excitement and anticipation into the big dip of culture shock and within six weeks I was very unhappy indeed. The reality of this loneliness and boredom took many years to go. Today, I know what to ask for, back then I did not even know the questions.

Q: What was most frustrating about your transition and why?

Having no company support, no one to turn to, no book to read and no resource. I was alone. The first spouse in my husband's company and so noone knew what to do with me.

Q: What freedoms did you find the most difficult to do without?

None. Dubai is free and easy. I could drive then. I could wear what I liked (within reason). I could get a job. I could join any club. I could move freely. It was easy. The only thing I missed was having a support network of family and friends I could call on. As I said, it was lonely.

Q: What outlets did you find worked best to remedy your frustration?

I used to go to the pool complex at our apartment block and began to make a few friends from the familiar faces there. I used to go out to the bar with my husband in his free time to meet his friends, even though they were mainly male, just so I could talk and ask questions. It did not take long before I met some other women: the wife of Ian's squash buddy, the people at the diving club, even the girl behind the bar, and things began to change. I am a natural networker, not that I even knew the phrase back then, and tell people what I do for a living (or would do if only I could find the work) and so it was not long before a connection from the bar asked me to write a CV for a local employment agency client and my first freelance work began to arrive.

I don't like sport, so that was not an obvious route for me – though it is for many. Back then I had no kids, so mother and toddler groups were not an option. Soon, being a writer, I started a writers' circle and that gave me new friends who shared my passion for words. When kids came along I got involved in a mother and toddler group and produced their newsletter for them and I was never short of a friend ever again.

Q: What kept you from being able to work upon your arrival? In retrospect what advice would you give to women that would like to work to avoid this hang-up?

Well, I got a stamp in my passport that said 'wife – not allowed to work' would you believe – I believed it and got pretty depressed about that. But then I saw that other women, wives too, were working and realised that I could work again easily, I just needed a work permit and so I set about getting myself one. Again, all it took was asking for help and asking the right questions to solve the problem.

Q: What resources did you use to solve your problem of employment once you were there?

Networking. Asking. And making sure people were very clear about what kind of work I could do – not just specifically helpful people, like those who ran companies, but anyone. It often happens that you don't get referrals from people in your direct network but from friends of friends, so it does not pay to be shy. You need to shout your skills from the rooftops.

Q: What resources did you use to build your social network? How important was building a social network to your well-being?

My passion for writing led to my most fulfilling network, first as the writers' circle organiser and later as a writing teacher. I love to cook, so would ask Ian to invite people he knew but I didn't round to dinner so I could at least meet people. That worked well. And, like I said, the local pool was a good place and also my husband's networks – he plays squash, dives and was in a rock band, so I tagged along!

Q: What is the one best overall tip/piece of advice you could give to a spouse joining a husband who's been offered an overseas contract?

Don't guess what it will be like as I did, get online and find out for sure, build your network before you go, and ensure you have some dates in your diary ready and waiting for you. When I came to Holland five years ago I had already carefully built a network here, I had run a few writing workshops and attended some professional business events. The first dates in my diary were to speak at several clubs in Holland. That was a great start, much better than being a wallflower.

Q: What is the one logistical 'must do' that you could advise?

Get online first. Find a club that interests you – for mothers, business women, women in health, male partners (yes, those groups exist too), writing, flower-arranging, ballooning, whatever, and ensure you get out of the house to attend meetings right away.

Q: How did the move affect you personal identity? How did it affect your ability to play a certain role and form relationships?

I felt I lost my identity completely and floundered for many years until I felt comfortable in my role as entrepreneur and mother. I hated being asked "what do you do?" and feeling compelled to use the word 'just' in my reply – "just a wife", "just a trailing spouse." I felt second class. This is not helped by the fact that spouses tend by default to be defined by their roles as a wife and a mother and people often forget to ask about career choices. It is easy to feel second class and invisible, if professional identity is as important to you as it was to me.

Q: How did the move affect the relationship between yourself and your husband? What problems did you encounter? How did you solve them?

For ten years I resented being wrenched from my identity and thriving business. Then, one day, I realised I had created a thriving portable career and a brand new, better, more exciting identity of an expat spouse, mother and entrepreneur and would not go back to the old ways for the world. The main problems, I guess were my bottled up (or not so bottled up) resentment and hating to feel I was always giving in, compromising and following. It took me until 1999 to realise that I had actually been very blessed and lucky. How did I solve them? Reading books like those by Robin Pascoe, attending great conferences like *Families in Global Transition*, and talking to others in my position so I realised I was not alone and learned tools to cope and understand, and importantly, to appreciate how very lucky I have been.

And here is the finished piece:

The 'Trailing Spouse' No Longer Need Be Such A Drag

by Stephanie Katz of www.expatarrivals.com

Blurb: With a greater network of access and an entire industry devoted to cushioning change for expats, those accompanying their other half overseas no longer need to dread the distance from their past life.

Pull Quote: Don't guess what it will be like as I did, get online and find out for sure, build your network before you go, and ensure you have some dates in your diary ready and waiting for you

Word Count: 1165

Back in 1987 Jo Parfitt was starry-eyed, smitten and on her way half way across the world to accompany the man she'd married to a place she'd fingered on a map once, and visited twice.

Her husband Ian had lived and worked in Dubai for two years prior, but Jo, mad with the edge of excitement, had made no prior preparations and had haphazardly let expectation fall to the wayside. She departed for the Middle East in a heady cloud of anticipation – antsy to begin her life in the romantic sphere of expatriate living.

But like so many before her, and so many still to come, Jo hadn't foreseen the degree of difficulty and the extent of both physical and psychological hardship that this kind of move involves.

Culture shock

"I moved rapidly from excitement and anticipation into the big dip of culture shock and within six weeks I was very unhappy indeed. The reality of this loneliness and boredom took many years to go. Today, I know what to ask for, back then I did not," she admits quite candidly.

Now well-published and the author of *A Career in Your Suitcase*, a book about the ins and outs of maintaining your professional identity while moving overseas, Jo is an expert in the art of the expat life and the antics of adaptation. Still, she began as part of the spousal school of past – those forced to play the role of the follower and forego individual aspirations and ambitions.

These 'trailing spouses', an affectionate nickname credited to Mary Bralove of the Wall Street Journal in 1981, often have little idea about how dramatically life can change when relocating internationally to support a partner's career.

Often they're charged with managing the logistics of finding a house, with opening bank accounts, and with arranging appropriate schooling while their other half is fully immersed in the complexities of a new career. Though starting a new job creates its own difficulties, it is still a relatively familiar process. Not to mention, expats employed abroad work alongside fellow expats and within a zone lined with the comfort of shared behaviour.

Trailing spouses seldom share this luxury and may have to spar openly with the big, bad monster of foreign culture. Language barriers, strange business etiquette, and in the case of the Middle East restrictive laws can be the cause of constant confusion and consternation.

These days though, relocation specialists and contract stipulations usually provide adequate provision for many of these more obvious factors. For the most part, accommodation, health insurance and some form of subsidized education should be settled prior to expat's arrival.

Still, the elimination of these stressful variables may only serve to further expose the true vulnerability of the trailing spouse's plight.

"Having no company support, no one to turn to, no book to read and no resource. I was alone," recounts Parfitt of her own struggle.

Restricted identity

The most pointed issue a trailing spouse must learn to deal with is the loss of identity and the subsequent period of reshape and remodelling that ensues in the new environment. As the trailing spouse leaves friends, family, a career path or an impassioned endeavour, priorities begin to shape shift and reordering them can become chaotic in its own right.

Co-authors of A Portable Identity, relocation coaches Debra Bryson and Charise Hoge explain the phenomenon as a four stage process.

"The trailing spouse goes through several alterations: first, by the decision to move; second, by the actual departure from her home country; third, by the entry into the foreign country; and, finally, by the addition of new roles and relationships in her life overseas."

This transition can result in feelings of resentment, disorientation, depression, boredom and extreme pessimism. When coupled with the problems of career abandonment, family issues, lack of support by the sponsoring employer and difficulties in maintaining meaningful work the mental landscape of the trailing spouse can become very rocky indeed.

But thanks to published accounts like that of Parfitt, expat coaches like Bryson and Hoge, and reliable research that proves just how pivotal partners can be, life for the trailing spouse no longer need be such a drag.

Contract issues

Brookfield Global Relocation Services found that approximately 86 percent of transferees that were relocated were accompanied by spouses or partners; numerous publications over the past 30 years have reported that the number one cause of an assignee breaking their contract was spousal unhappiness; and according to the 2010 Corporate Relocations Survey by Atlas, 40 percent of firms say that a spouse/partner's employment "almost always" or "frequently" affects an employee's relocation.

Such hard figures are even harder to ignore, thus relocation assistance addressing the physical needs of the trailing spouse in conjunction with those of the assignee is being increasingly used as a recruitment tactic. Some companies have taken to arranging job interviews for the spouse, flying the whole family back and forth for reconnaissance visits and even helping in the moving process.

Assignees shouldn't be afraid to demand this type of attention, and should go as far as to make relevant inclusions in their contract.

Preparing in advance of working

Negotiating a work permit as a trailing spouse can be an issue that makes or breaks relocation.

"Spouses tend by default to be defined in their roles of partner and caregiver and people often forget to ask about career choices. It is easy to feel second-class and invisible, if professional identity is as important to you as it was to me," explains Parfitt.

Obtaining a work permit is just one piece to the greater puzzle of taking charge of the changes associated with the mobile lifestyle and turning challenges into opportunities.

The most important thing a trailing spouse should do to take control of the expat experience is to prepare.

"Don't guess what it will be like as I did, get online and find out for sure, build your network before you go, and ensure you have some dates in your diary ready and waiting for you," recommends Parfitt.

Take advantage of all the resources available to find clubs, interest groups and information-dense expat websites such as www.expatarrivals.com. Making the necessary contacts in advance is very viable thanks to social media tools such as LinkedIn and expat bulletin boards and forums. Trailing spouses can also start by getting in touch with the local Chamber of Commerce, by registering with various employment agencies and by networking with friends, families your partner's employer and other expats in the area.

Otherwise take the necessary steps to keep busy; donate time to non-profit organizations, further your studies or invest time in a hobby you've always wanted to pursue.

As a trailing spouse it's vital to take the steps necessary to create a mindset that's meaningful; reassert your identity as something portable, transient and more respectable and enriched than ever before.

For more information about expat life and for valuable information about what to expect from a destination visit www.expatarrivals.com.

Recipe for a case study or profile

You will likely often find yourself writing about people in your features articles. Over the years I have profiled many people, usually interviewing them about their careers. Each time I have used this recipe because it works. A case study or profile will typically be based on a short interview by email or face to face. I use just four ingredients:

- Introduction
- Quotation
- Expansion
- Conclusion

Take a look at the piece below that was written after a short interview with Shabnam Yussuf about her portable career. See how each section belongs to one of the ingredients above.

'A healthy alternative'

Shabnam Yussuf is of Indian origin yet also has British and Swiss passports. She has moved frequently as an adult, having lived in the UK, USA, Thailand, Yugoslavia, France, India, Bali and is now in Switzerland. Originally trained in Ayurveda and Homeopathy she has now added Magnetotherapy and Nutrition to her toolbox. Shabnam currently works in a private practice with her Swiss husband as what is called a Bioacoustics Practitioner.

} Introduct

"Beginning anew every time is difficult, especially when you work in an area such as alternative healthcare," explains Shabnam. "I also work with some methods that are considered a bit 'weird and wacky' by some people, such as Thought Field Therapy and Infra Sounds. Introducing new concepts into a new country brings another challenge."

} Quotatio

She has also found that the fact that she belongs to a minority group and is a different colour from the Swiss with whom she works that this can be another barrier.

} Expansio

"I have learned that it never works if I try to become more like the locals than the locals themselves. Being different can work in my favour once people know me. It is better to be proud of your origins, while respecting local traditions. Discrimination is only the result of fear stemming from the unknown and therefore I do not take it personally. After all, under the skin and traditions, people are the same everywhere."

} Quotatio

Fortunately, Shabnam has discovered that she has increased her chances of running a successful business by focusing on the expatriate community. Here, where everyone is different for one reason or another, it is easier to blend in.

} Conclusi

270 words

The recipe for a case study could be:

1. Introduction of piece
2. Quote
3. Introduction of new topic
4. Quote
5. Extension of topic
6. Quote
7. And so on until...
8. Conclusion

Research

Research will add depth to your article. See if you can obtain quotes from relevant people, professionals and case studies. It is often easy to do this over the telephone or by email or Skype.

As I said earlier, study the style and layout the editor seems to like. Check article length and stick to it. Study the advertisements again too. They are placed carefully to appeal to the magazine's readership, so they tell you more about the kind of readers you are writing for. Now you can slant your article towards their interests.

When researching your topic always jot down where you found any quotes or figures. The editor may need to double-check the facts. Just in case anyone ever tries to deny that they said what you said they said, you must hold onto the transcripts of your interviews for three years.

HOMEWORK ASSIGNMENT FOUR

STEP ONE

Take a look at the *Woman Abroad* guidelines that I gave you in Lesson Three.

STEP TWO

Create an outline of an article for this magazine, one that is honed to the publication. You can take an idea from the list you made for Lesson One, or, if you have had a new idea, then that is also fine.

Please include:

- Title
- Standfirst/leader/slug sentence
- Short paragraph description of the piece just as you would write it if you were selling it to me, the editor. Ensure you tell me to whom you would talk for quotes or case studies and what you would put in the sidebars.

STEP THREE

Create a new document in Word and use it to submit your assignment.

Name your document with your name, DA (for *Definite Articles*) and the lesson number. So, if your name is Mary Smith you would name your file MarySmithDA4.

Send this document to your personal tutor by email who will then mark it and send it back to you within two weeks.

Now you can start reading and working with Lesson Five. However, do not submit the homework for the next Lesson Five until you have received your critique for Lesson Four.

SAMPLE HOMEWORK FOUR

Susan submitted the following homework assignment.

Title:

'Soaring as a Trailing Spouse'

Leader:

Susan Adkins explores the ideal attributes of a trailing expatriate spouse.

Opening Paragraph:

The term 'trailing spouse' evokes an image of something being drug through the dust. My own experiences and observations have convinced me that the opposite is true: Any woman can use her husband's work assignment abroad as a launching pad to personal and professional fulfillment and to forging deeper connections with her spouse and children.

Outline:

Overview of the challenges facing trailing spouses:

- Settler International, a worldwide relocation assistance company reports that 'The divorce rate among expatriate couples is 40 percent higher than their domestic counterparts'.
- Specific examples of challenges faced by trailing spouses
- Personal anecdotes
- Profile of the book *A Portable Identity: A Woman's Guide to Maintaining a Sense of Self While Moving Overseas*

Personality of the Perfect Mobile Wife

- Overview of 'Ideal Traits'
- Pre-assignment selection process
- Quotes from the Community Liaison Officer at the U.S. Embassy in The Hague.

What Companies and Working Spouses Can Do to Help

- Overview of what can be done
- Quotes from family counselor

Opportunities for the Trailing Spouse

- Overview of career possibilities and the opportunity of personal development for the trailing spouse

Conclusion:

A woman who chooses to support her husband in a career move that takes the family overseas has already displayed two key characteristics of an ideal expatriate wife: courage and an adventurous soul. Change is always difficult, but once she learns to open up to the possibilities her new life presents her, she is no longer trailing – she is soaring!

Sidebar:

- What Makes the 'Perfect Expatriate Wife'? (Surprise: you fit the description!) List of 5 key qualities.
- Presentation on the trailing spouse conducted by Yvonne McNulty and is available at:
  http://www.thetrailingspouse.com/docs/Trailing_Spouse_Presentation_FIGT_March_2004.pdf
- *A Portable Identity: A Woman's Guide to Maintaining a Sense of Self While Moving Overseas* by Debra R. Bryson and Charise M. Hoge is published by Transition Press International and is available at:
  www.aportableidentity.com
- *A Moveable Marriage: Relocate Your Marriage Without Breaking It* and *A Broad Abroad: An Expat Wife's Guide to Successful Living Abroad*, both by Robin Pascoe and published by Expatriate Press Limited. They are available at:
  www.expatexpert.com/bookstore
- *A Career in Your Suitcase* by Jo Parfitt is published by Lean Marketing Press and is available at:
  www.joparfitt.com
- *Realities of Foreign Service Life, Volume 2* by Patricia Linderman, Melissa Brayer Hess and Marlene Monfiletto Nice and published by iUniverse, inc. It is available at:
  www.amazon.com

LESSON FIVE

Beginnings, middles and ends

When you sell an article you are actually selling an idea. Your writing style may not always be the deciding factor. What you write about is what matters. This lesson will cover the way to write the key sections of your article. It will cover what you could put into those sections and help you to see that you have a lot of choice.

To start with let's look at the 'ingredients' you can include in your article in more detail.

The ingredients

I like to think of the elements you could use in an article as 'ingredients'. There are many options here, and you are unlikely to use them all in every piece, but the following will give you some ideas:

1. Title to intrigue the reader

2. Leader (with your name in it)

3. Opening paragraph to set the scene
    a. Statistic/survey result (with source)
    b. Quotation from expert or case study or book (with source)
    c. Question
    d. Fact
    e. Observation
    f. Anecdote (personal or third person)

4. Middle
    a. Case studies. Use one to three, ideally and try to vary the types of interviewee to allow for a balanced view. If you were going to write about portable careers in France perhaps, you should talk to three people who are all very different.
    b. Quotations from the people you interviewed for case studies
    c. Short quotes from experts/books/Internet (with source)
    d. Expansion or information on the topic discussed
    e. Bullet-pointed lists
    f. Subheadings
    g. Personal anecdote

h. More facts
i. More statistics
j. More survey results

5. End
   a. Conclusion, wrap up, refer back to earlier comments, new insight related to previous text

6. Sidebars (added value)
   a. Exercise
   b. Quiz
   c. Tips (5 tips for/10 tips for/7secrets to/ 5 ways to)
   d. Further reading (book title, author, publisher)
   e. Related websites
   f. Travel related information where to stay, how to get there
   g. Websites or books from those experts quoted in the piece
   h. Related conferences, date and URL
   i. Related products
   j. Related information in bullet form

7. Your name (byline)

8. Your biography – short with name of company or website, if encouraged by the publication

Opening paragraphs

The best opening paragraphs are short and to the point. They should consist of words that hook the browsing reader's attention instantly, with a promise of what is to come. Dated perhaps, but who could resist the invitation to read on after Austen's tongue-in-cheek opening to *Pride and Prejudice*: 'It is a truth universally acknowledged, that a single man in possession of a good fortune, must be in want of a wife.' The same is true for non-fiction. The first paragraph of M. Scott Peck's *The Road Less Travelled* is: 'Life is difficult.' Compelling, isn't it?

Readers have a shorter attention span than ever. TV, DVDs, podcasts, vodcasts, and the Internet offer instant, visual, less demanding attractions. Getting the opening lines of an article right has never been more important.

Golden rules

- Make sure your opening paragraph is uncomplicated and without sub-clauses winding their way through the sentences that distract attention away from the main idea.

- Look for something unexpected, controversial or unusual to mention if you can.

- Read your first paragraph aloud. It will make it easier to spot any errors.

- The ideal opening paragraph hones in on a single idea, scene or proposition. Look at the information you have for your feature, or think carefully about what you want to say, and pull out the most interesting angle or thought. Sometimes it's good to quote a fact or statistic, though bear in mind that most editors will want you to state the source of your statistics.

- Don't spend too long on your opening paragraph. I find it is easier to write it last, after I've completed the whole piece.

Here are some of my own, published, opening paragraphs:

Going Global

Advances in technology have given rise to cries of 'Live Local Work Global'. However, for today's senior managers, nothing can replace the real thing. If you want to 'work global' you need a taste of living globally too.

Managing a Career Break

People take career breaks for a variety of reasons. Bringing up a family is the most common, but it is not unusual to take a break for travel or study, to pursue sporting ambitions or simply to take time out, reassess personal motivations and set new objectives.

International Job Hunting

When your grass is too wet to mow for the second weekend in a row and you're sick of commuting, going to live abroad can seem like a brilliant idea. Finding a job abroad has never been easier and right now 10 million Britons are overseas, with Europe, the USA and Australia being the most popular destinations.

The Demise of the Dogsbody

The days of traditional apprenticeships in engineering or craft industries are gone and while many bemoan their demise, the dogsbodies of the past are laughing all the way to their diplomas. Apprenticeships that had young men earning a pittance and working long hours have now changed beyond recognition. They not only include most types of industry, they are now also open to women.

Mothers in Management

In the past decade the UK's employee satisfaction level has dropped by a greater percentage than any other European country. At the same time, the sickness absence rates have risen to hit an all-time high of £12 billion cost to industry in one year.

Making an Overseas Assignment Work For You

The October 2000 Global Relocation Trends Survey has just been published. Of the 154 companies interviewed, with/canvassing 52,000 employees in 43 worldwide locations, the highest percentage of companies surveyed are involved in high-tech and IT fields.

Human-interest/Opening with a personal touch

Women's magazines like the human angle in any story. So this is a good occasion to put a person in the first paragraph.

Janice Redman looked out of the broken windowpane and watched the ferry sail away to Norway. Now she would never be able to find her Viking ancestors...

Use a leader

Many features articles will include a *leader* paragraph that, as mentioned in Lesson Four, sums up the content of the feature. These leader paragraphs are called many different things including *sell*, *slug*, *standfirst* and *blurb*.

My husband lives next door – with her

Maureen was happy to let her neighbour borrow the odd pinta ... but drew the line at lending her husband, as Fiona Hudson discovered.

Glancing through the curtains, Maureen Birch saw a removal van pull up opposite her home. 'Ooh, look John!' she called excitedly to her husband. 'Our new neighbours have arrived.'

Leaders used to be written by editors, but time is increasingly precious these days and your editor will be grateful if you have done it already.

See whether your magazine puts the author's name (byline) in the leader or not and make sure you do the same!

Beginnings

The first paragraph is of great importance. It must grip the editor's and reader's attention immediately. It is often useful to select a particularly juicy piece of information and start with that. This can be even more effective if the information is turned into a quote. See if you can use any statistics, such as "a recent survey by Oil Co. has shown that while 75 per cent of accompanying partners on expatriate assignment want to work while abroad, just 25 per cent actually succeed."

The best opening paragraphs are short and to the point. They are accurate. Just 30-50 words is good. More is fine if it is well crafted. Words that hook the browsing reader's attention and tell you what you are going to read about are best of all.

Keep sentence construction as short and uncomplicated as you can.

Use plain vocabulary and everyday English.

Look for something unexpected. If the subject of your feature article is a mother of four who works on a building site, or works in a registry office but has never married her husband, use that.

Only use quotations if they are compelling.

Avoid clichés. Only use them if they can be used satirically. For example, don't call an article on cheesecakes *Just desserts* but do call an article on Arabia *Just deserts*.

When you have written your first paragraph read it out loud and put yourself in the shoes of the reader. Does it still work?

Break rules if necessary of course. Everyone has a different style, but your style must be appropriate to the magazine's readers. Remember to check the magazine you want to write for first.

The ideal opening paragraph hones in on a single idea or scene. Try to pull out the most interesting angle or thought.

Here are the title, leader and opening paragraph of a piece that appeared in the *Weekly Telegraph*.

A Career in Settling-in Services

Wouldn't it be wonderful if you could create a career based simply on where you are living and what and whom you know? Jo Parfitt discovers this may be the perfect job for some expatriates.

Many expatriate wives who do not work while they are abroad consider that the longer they stay abroad, the more unemployable they become. They fail to recognise that simply by being familiar with local day-to-day routines, they are acquiring a valuable skill that can easily be converted into a reasonably well-paid, flexible career.

Middles

The middle must fulfil the promise of that good first paragraph. Move logically from one thought to the next. This is where you put your quotations, anecdotal evidence, case studies and ideas. Each time you use dialogue make sure to start a new paragraph. Take a look at the style of the publication you are aiming for. How do they lay out their speech?

Here is the start of one of my articles that was published in the *Weekly Telegraph* in 2002.

> ### *Paradise Postponed*
>
> Many of us dream of buying a tumbledown house in France, which we will enjoy doing up over a series of summers, in the hope of retiring there one day. Paul and Julia Herbert and their three children, Samantha (8), Jay (6) and Ryan (3) bought one such house 10 years ago, in a little hamlet just north of Perigueux, in the Dordogne. But then Paul lost almost everything the family owned through litigation with a former employer, which went horribly wrong. Everything that is, but a derelict French farmhouse and a few hundred pounds.
>
> 'I can remember arriving just before midnight in pouring rain, my children crying that they wanted to go home. It isn't easy explaining to a three year old who has been used to a large luxurious house, that his new home is run down and smelly, and where the only running water is that which is coming in through the roof,' recalls Paul.
>
> 'I felt numb, angry, helpless, useless, inadequate, sick to my stomach. Who in their right mind would uproot their children and take them to a foreign country where they did not speak the language, without any money and no real means of support? I was running away from the shame.'
>
> That first summer, the Herberts eked out some kind of a living selling the £1500 worth of children's clothes they had taken with them to sell on the local market. When the tourists went home, their market dried up. Paul has a photograph of Winston Churchill in his office, and the saying "never give in". Despite great difficulties, the Herberts have never given in.

In the example, above, the dialogue starts a new paragraph each time. Also notice that the 'recipe' above is introduction, quote, quote, expansion.

If your target publication breaks up the text with subheadings and ensure yours does the same.

Introducing experts and case studies

It is worth mentioning at this point the method I favour for introducing the people you will quote from during your article. These are the people you have spoken to and interviewed for your piece. They may be the authors whose short extracts you are quoting. They may be the people whose quotes that you Quote Spotted for during a talk or seminar. In each case you will need to ensure the reader knows exactly who these people are and how they fit in to your article.

I like to introduce the person in full, so the reader is absolutely clear who he or she is and then end that paragraphs. I then start a new paragraph with the quote, blending a phrase including 'he says', 'writes Roberts', 'she continued' or whatever into that paragraph. Below are some fictitious examples. Notice in the third one how I used italics for a book title. See in all the examples how fully each person is introduced.

Jane Brown runs the online network called Whizz, which now boasts 12,000 members. She ran a seminar on the importance of social media marketing at a Network to Win conference in Prague in June 2010.

"Time was, the size of your social network was the size of your Christmas cards list," said Brown. "Today, many people will have connections through online social networks that run into the thousands. It is time to wake up to Whizz."

Or

Bob and Sue Thorne are British and have lived in Dubai for three years now with their pre-school twin boys who were born there. Sue is now pregnant again and will have the baby in London.

"The hospitals here are first rate and I would have no hesitation in giving birth here this time too. Jack and Joe have beautiful Arabic birth certificates and it was easy to register them with the British Embassy. However, if either of them chooses to have a baby outside the UK themselves, that baby may have a problem retaining British citizenship. That's why I'm going home," Sue explains.

Or

Ruth van Reken is the co-author of *Third Culture Kids: Growing Up Among Worlds*, published by Nicholas Brealey Intercultural. She is a specialist in the issues that surround cross-cultural children and transition and believes that one way to help a child to settle in a new country is to make setting up a real home a priority.

"I'll never forget my father's words each time we moved to a new city in Africa," she writes. "Unpack your bags and plant your trees, he would say. And he was right."

Ends

Tie up all loose ends, positively if possible. Perhaps you could look to the future or go back to a question posed at the beginning. Avoid a recap of the text. Don't bring in any new information. You could leave the reader with a strong point to ponder over.

The *'Mothers in Management'* piece, mentioned earlier, ended with this:

Steps are already underway to amalgamate MIM with Parents at Work, thereby adopting a mother-free name.

"Mothers have been indoctrinated to put themselves last, feeling guilty if they put themselves first," said Ms Conran. "It's about time we stopped feeling so guilty and started being selfish," she advised.

Sidebars

Mothers in Management can be contacted on 0171 628 2128
Parents at Work can be contacted on 0171 628 3565

The *'Managing a Career Break'* piece ended like this:

Nigel Gardner decided to take a career break from his position as a Financial Director last May. Part of the terms of his resignation was that his company provide him with job search training. He chose to join an outplacement scheme with Executive Action who specialise in supporting people at director level.

Nigel did not start out with a clear direction for his new career, but has developed a strategy, with the aid of Executive Action, to target small- to medium-sized growing companies who might need his financial/administrative skills through networking and selective mailshots. Gardner says 'Executive Action have helped in many areas and have been very supportive, but, with hindsight, I needed to spend more time developing my selling skills.'

Sidebars

CEPEC 0171 629 2266
Executive Action 0171 299 2900
Women in Accountancy, President, Anne Jenkins tel/fax – 0181-287-4003;
Email – Anne.Jenkins@virgin.net

'Paradise Postponed' ended like this:

> Paul puts his success down to having a wife who he regularly calls 'his rock', the recommendations they continue to receive from satisfied holidaymakers, a team of company directors and staff who are 100 per cent dedicated, and to "sheer blood and guts".
>
> *Sidebars*
>
> If you would like to find out more about Paul and Julia's business please look at www.franceonecall.com, www.bonjourmagazine.com, www.onecallestates.com or email queries to Paul@franceonecall.com. A franchise to the onecall scheme costs £15,000, which includes website and marketing support.

Dialogue

Dialogue gives an article sparkle. Quotes are effective and draw the reader into the story. They don't have to be very long and of course you can reword the actual words a little if the speakers were ungrammatical, so long as you don't change the meaning. It's a good idea to get the speaker's approval once you have tweaked the words.

Don't worry about using the words 'he said' and 'she said' too often. In an article, most readers don't even notice such words. Often it can be better to use 'said' than 'muttered', 'gasped' or 'interjected'. The article will look more interesting if the dialogue starts a new paragraph each time.

Making it come alive

Lengthy descriptions or lists of facts make unexciting reading. If you have lots of facts save them for a sidebar. Put in the names of people, anecdotes, real-life experiences, pertinent descriptions, movement, action and so on. For a lightweight publication, readers will want to know if the subjects are married, and the names of their children. In a business publication, only use this information if it is relevant.

Style

Although everyone has their own style, it is useful to remember that short sentences speed up the pace. Try not to repeat yourself. Use *you* rather than *I* to bring the reader closer to the story and its characters. Vary sentence length according to content. Vary sentence construction. Try to keep paragraphs short. Long words, unless appropriate, do not impress. Keep it simple. Never use three words when two will do. Never use a three syllable word when a shorter one will do.

Don't use foreign words unless you put them in italics. Don't make your reader feel stupid; explain things if necessary.

Sidebars

If you are researching, say, the validity of the health farm, you should consider including a list of health farms, their prices and services, for example. Editors appreciate this. In the examples given above you can see some of the kinds of useful information to put in a sidebar.

Examples

If you want to see some examples of articles that I have written please take a look at my website www.joparfitt.com or at the *Expat Telegraph* website www.telegraph.co.uk or www.expatica.com/hr. Alternatively, simply key 'Jo Parfitt' into a search engine to find countless examples of my work.

Getting the article published

Many people think that the way to be a freelance article writer is to have an idea, write a piece and then send it off to potential publications, one at a time. Sadly, this is a misconception. Writing the article is the *last* thing you do.

In reality the first step is to have an idea and find an appropriate market for that idea.

The next step is to understand what that publication and its readers will want and to hone your idea for that. It is a good idea to look at the *writers' guidelines* at this point.

The next step is to pitch that idea to the publication. Within the outline explain which experts you will contact for quotations, if appropriate, and whom you may contact for anecdotal evidence.

And then, if they like your idea they will send you a *brief* as to the exact topic, word count and the deadline by which they would like you to have written and submitted it.

Upon being commissioned, produce an interesting and well-written article that adheres to the contributors' guidelines and the editor's brief exactly. If you are not given a brief, ask for one. It is easy to misunderstand what the editor wants and you might end up having to rewrite your article. A brief avoids this, although not all magazines issue them.

Now you can send your article to the editor.

Here is a typical brief for you to look at:

Article brief

Working title: Expat house husbands

Length: 8000 characters (circa 1400 words), including fact file

Deadline: 20 January 2002

I'd like you to do an interview piece about one or more male spouses from a different country or cultural background than that of their wives.

Basically, I'd like to set an example for women who are thinking of accepting an overseas job offer, as well as their partners, that things can work out this way, too. Another point is to give male spouses ideas (and contacts) for networking.

Points for discussion could include:

• How these men came to choose 'foreign' wives?

• Was this a difficult decision for them? Did it mean having to take a break from working life and become 'house husbands'?

• Do they feel that they are somehow treated differently from non-national women married to local men, and if so, how does this manifest and can they give examples?

• What kinds of social networks do they have?

• What do they see as the positive sides of a) being from a different country and b) perhaps staying at home while their spouses go to work?

• What are the difficult aspects of life as a foreign spouse?

Usually our interview pieces include a fact file of the interviewee (nationality, occupation, where they live at the moment, where they've lived before,

---

family, career turns, hobbies), but if you are going to interview a group of people, it might be a good idea to skip the fact files this time.

Also, try not to include references to current events or anything that would become out of date quickly, as the reading time for each issue is about three months.

My students are frequently surprised when they learn that writing the article itself is not the first step. So let me recap on the process, here, below:

Seven steps to getting your article in print

1. Have a good idea for a subject.

2. Find a suitable market (or publication).

3. Read some recent back issues.

4. Write a pitch email that will attract the editor's attention and send it. (We'll cover this in Lesson Seven)

5. Await the commission to write your article.

6. Write your articles.

7. Submit a professional looking manuscript, by email, as an attachment together with sidebars, author bio and illustrations.

The writing process

Once you have had your idea, pitched it and received a commission you can now start to research and prepare for your article, conduct any interviews and write it. And even then, you will need to polish and fine-tune it further. I am a firm believer in the value of feedback too.

Indeed, there are many steps to writing an article, so here is the way I do it:

Fifteen steps to a final draft of your article

1.   Decide whom to interview.

2.   Conduct your interviews.

3.   Decide what extra research you need to do – maybe to source facts, statistics, quotes from books or from experts in the field.

4.   Obtain the information you need from your research.

5.   Write a first draft straight onto the computer, without much editing or stopping. Start with the beginning, move onto the middle, then write the end.

6.   Read the piece aloud. Correct any howlers or errors and amend the structure or order in which you give information. I usually find that the first and last paragraphs are the toughest – so worry about them last.

7.   Edit the piece.

8.   Write the title.

9.   Write the leader.

10.   Compose the sidebars.

---

11.   Write your author bio.

12.   Ask a third party to comment.

13.   Amend again. Read aloud again. Polish again. Check the spelling of all names, resource information and so on.

14.   Print and check again. It looks different on the printed page.

15.   Do a word count. Add the words 'word count xx' at the very start or end of the piece. The word count will include all the extra text, such as title, leader and sidebars.

Just because you have lots of information is no reason to use it all in one article – stretch it to make several different articles.

HOMEWORK ASSIGNMENT FIVE

Let's get into practice! I am now going to give you a brief for an article for a fictitious magazine.

I do not expect you to do the actual research for this or to write it. This homework is about your struture and outline. If you want to do this piece for real and write it in its entirety then please feel free to do so. But if you are happy to make stuff up and invent your experts and expats that too is fine. If you do it for real, then this will really be a great exercise.

STEP ONE

Find a magazine or website that you would like to write for someday. Have an idea for a piece and prepare an outline that will allow you tshows you have thought about the beginning, the middle and the end, the people you will interview and the sidebars.

STEP TWO

Submit an outline for your article according to the guide below:

1. Name the target publication.
2. Write a title.
3. Write a leader that includes your name/byline.
4. Write the complete opening paragraph.
5. Write an outline of the content of the middle of the article with subheadings if required. You will not write this section – merely give me the bare bones of your ideas.
6. Write the complete closing paragraph.
7. Include some sidebar information.

STEP THREE

Create a new document in Word and use it to submit your assignment.

Name your document with your name, DA (for Definite Articles) and the lesson number. So, if your name is Mary Smith you would name your file MarySmithDA5.

Send this document to your personal tutor by email who will then mark it and send it back to you within two weeks.

Now you can start reading and working with Lesson Six. However, do not submit the homework for the next Lesson Six until you have received your critique for Lesson Five.

HOMEWORK SAMPLE FIVE

Rebecca submitted the following homework sample.

Target publication: American in Britain magazine

Title: *Kids on the Move*

Leader:

Taking our children overseas with us can overwhelm us with guilt and worry. Rebecca Pauley explains how to manage their expectations and make the most of a great opportunity.

Opening paragraph:

Yesterday eleven-year-old Eric Johnson cried at school. He recently moved to Sussex from Illinois, with his parents and elder siblings, Elliot and Anne. Eric was crying because he was being teased for being American.

Outline:

- Overview of the situation for third culture kids (expat kids).

- Specific example of what classmates say to Eric in school.

- Case studies of three parents and how they handle their expat kids. Each family living in a different part of the UK.

- Personal anecdote of own expat kids, with quotes.

- Mention the Third Culture Kid Profile book *Third Culture Kids*.

- Personal story from Michelle Thumper (now 21), who was a TCK.

- Psychologists' advice with quotes.

- Examples of products and training available to help TCKs and their parents.

Conclusion:

The happiness of our children matters because if they do not adjust to your overseas posting, then you will be unhappy too. And if you, the parents, continue to be unhappy then you are unlikely to remain abroad. The employer will lose a key employee as well as the associated potential revenue. The cost to the company is likely to be well in excess of £100,000. But what price would you, the parent, put on your child's happiness?

Sidebar:

Third Culture Kids: The Experience of Growing Up Among Worlds by David Pollock and Ruth E Van Reken is published by Nicholas Brealey/Intercultural Press and is available from www.interculturalpress.com.
Families on the Move by Marion Knell is published by Monarch Books and is available from www.globalconnections.co.uk.
Let's Move Overseas and *Footsteps Around the World* by Beverley Roman are published by BR Anchor and available from www.branchor.com.
Let's Move Together by Carol Shubeck is published by Suitcase Press and available from cmshubeck@aol.com.
Your Move and all Transitional Learning Curve products are available from www.transitionallearning.com.
Living and Working Abroad – a Parent's Guide by Robin Pascoe is available from www.expatexpert.com.

LESSON SIX

Be Your Own Editor

Customising tips

Writers must customise their copy so that it fits the magazine for which it is destined. Sub-editors are disappearing or are short of time and your copy will often be taken as it was sent to the magazine for immediate use. If the sub-editor notices right away that your article is going to be hard to edit, there is a chance that it will still be rejected. A busy editor will be daunted by text that uses double quotes when single are the house style, or American spelling when British was asked for.

Even if an article has been commissioned, this is no cast-iron guarantee that it will be used. Sometimes it may be held back for a future issue, even a year or more away. Sometimes the late sale of an advert means that your piece has to be cut considerably or not used at all. If you have not quite adhered to your brief, this could turn your commission into a rejection.

On occasion I have been commissioned to write a piece and been given an unclear brief. The editor knew exactly what *she* wanted, and I knew exactly what *I thought* she wanted. However, the misunderstanding resulted in my piece being massacred, or not used at all. If you are ever in doubt, double-check that you have the focus right before you start to work. If you want to increase your chances of being used again, make sure your first submission is as perfect as can be. Make it easy for the editor and you will become a popular contributor.

- Before you start writing, look at the contributors' guidelines for any notes on the house style. Notice whether the magazine uses full stops after titles, such as Dr or Mrs. When you create a list, does the magazine use bullet points for each point? Does the first word of a list have a capital letter? Does each list entry finish with a full stop? Do they capitalise words like 'Summer'? Do they use full words or numbers for numerals? It tends to be standard to write figures in words up to and including nine, and then in figures after that. So, for example, you could have the phrase "Please bring along between three and 12 samples of your work."

- If your target market is a magazine that favours anecdotal pieces notice how they deal with names. Some may say "my friend Lucy" others may say "Lucy Beckwith", others "Lucy Beckwith, a teacher from Luton." Once Lucy Beckwith has been first introduced, is she later referred to as "Lucy", "Beckwith" or "Ms Beckwith"?

- Make sure your characters are involved with 'labels' the reader can identify with. Someone in *Country Living* would wear Jaeger and drive a Land Rover. Someone in *Bella* would wear clothes from a high street fashion store favoured by teens and be learning to drive a Ford Ka.

- Add softness to pieces for women's magazines, leave serious stuff for papers.

- Add sidebars and do your own titles and leaders according to the magazine's style.

- Put yourself in the shoes of the reader. Think about the TV shows she/he watches, the food, clothes and car she/he buys and how they bring up their children. You do not want to alienate or patronise the readers, so make sure you pitch your story at the appropriate level.

- Think about illustrations and either suggest or provide some of your own. It is standard to supply photos as digital JPEG files.

Cutting

Many years ago, before I had even thought of being a journalist, I overheard a conversation that would stay with me forever. A man, clad from head to toe in motorcycle leathers, was standing in our driveway. Rupert was the editor of a motorcycle magazine and a colleague of my brother's. My father had just given up a career as a teacher to become a full-time writer and had buttonholed Rupert before he had reached our front door.

"Hey Rupert, may I have a word?" asked my father, who had heard the approaching motorbike and was already walking across the gravel drive in his slippers.

"Sure," he said, taking off his helmet.

"If you had just one piece of advice to give to a new journalist, what would it be?" my father asked.

"Cut, cut and cut again," advised Rupert. "Oh, and never use a long word where a short word would do."

It is common during a first draft to use far more words than are necessary. It is typical for me to turn a 1000 word first draft into a 700 word article. It is amazing how much of what we write is superfluous. It is also easy to think that we will impress readers and editors by using long words. Unless you are aiming for a literary magazine the opposite is true. Using difficult vocabulary will alienate some readers. It is vital that your style is accessible. They say you should write at a level that would be understood by a 13 year-old child if you want to acquire a simple, flowing style.

Never use a three syllable word where a two or even one would do. Perhaps, instead of writing 'at this moment in time', you could write 'now'. Instead of 'xenophobic', write 'hates foreigners'. Try using 'lucky' instead of 'fortunate'. Of course there are exceptions. If you know your readers probably know what a xenophobe is, then go ahead and use the word. But be careful.

If you use a string of polysyllabic words, the chances are that the sentence will become hard to digest. I nearly wrote 'rather hard to digest' here, but stopped myself. The word 'rather' is superfluous.

Similarly, don't write 'at the very end of the corridor' but 'at the end of the corridor'.

Forget words like *really*. They're superfluous.

Take out a word and if the sentence still means the same, leave it out.

Stick to short words, short sentences, short paragraphs. Try to cut long sentences in half in order to avoid sub paragraphs or brackets. In general brackets are not favoured. See whether your magazine uses a dash – rather than brackets – to indicate a sub clause. But, in general, try to avoid sub clauses altogether (if you can manage it).

Test out your writing by reading it aloud. If you find yourself stumbling when you recite, then you will also stumble over words when you read silently. I call this kind of text 'clunky'. Just as an old road can be full of potholes, lumps and bumps, so can a long, winding sentence full of long words. Reading aloud could be your saviour.

Exclamation marks should usually be avoided too. I hate them! I think they cheapen the text considerably! But if your target market likes its brackets and its exclamation marks go ahead and use them. Personally, I think they show laziness and maybe immaturity on the part of the writer.

Dialogue

Keep dialogue sharp too. In real life we mumble, repeat ourselves and say 'er' a lot. You will need to cut this kind of waffle out. Notice how publications write dialogue. Most tend to do this:

"I hate running uphill," said Jane.

Rather than:

Jane said: "I hate running uphill."

Writing dialogue accurately was one of the hardest things for me to master, and it took lots of practice and referring back to other articles before it came naturally. It can be difficult to decide how to introduce an expert when you are using one of their quotes. There are several ways to do this:

Method one

Sandra Webb has 12 years in personnel management. She now offers a range of services, from job-search preparation to working for small companies as an ad hoc personnel manager.

"Everybody who employs someone at some time will have an employee issue and there is so much red tape and legislation around that it can be hard for small business owners to keep up to date," says Ms Webb.

Method two

"Everybody who employs someone at some time will have an employee issue and there is so much red tape and legislation around that it can be hard for small business owners to keep up to date," says Sandra Webb, who has 12 years experience in personnel management. Ms Webb currently offers a range of services, from job-search preparation to working for small companies as an ad hoc personnel manager.

Method three

"Everybody who employs someone at some time will have an employee issue," says Sandra Webb, who has 12 years experience in personnel management. "There is so much red tape and legislation around that it can

be hard for small business owners to keep up to date." Ms Webb currently offers a range of services, from job-search preparation to working for small companies as an ad hoc *personnel manager.*

Notice that it is quite common not to repeat the 'he said'/'she said' tags after dialogue. If the same person is speaking then this will be understood.

You are not obliged to show your finished article to any of the people you may have interviewed. However, some people can be sticky customers, and it may be in your interest to show them the copy. If they ask to see your work, I suggest that you only send them the section that refers to them. Say that if you do not have the comments within 24 hours you will assume it is acceptable. There is nothing worse than having to delay submitting your copy because an interviewee fails to get back to you.

Presentation

Again, look at the contributors' guidelines for rules on how to present your final manuscript. You are likely to be asked to double-space the text and add page numbers. Have good margins too.

In maybe 99 per cent of cases, you'll be expected to submit your articles as an email attachment in Word. A few magazines prefer the article to be pasted into the email because they have problems with attachments. Few magazines expect copy to be submitted by post. Editors are always busy, so if they can make changes on screen and then send the piece directly to be laid out on the page, this will save time. When I worked as an editor I was horrified when a piece was submitted on paper, as it was down to me to type it in if I was going to use it.

Include a word count. Put your name in the footer on every page, as well as the article title. Maybe like this:

Joanna Parfitt
26 Forane
4033 Forus
Stavanger
Norway
Tel 0047-51575207
Email jo@joparfitt.com

Housegirls Make You Fat
Joanna Parfitt

1,251 words

Joanna Parfitt explains why having help in the house was no help to her waistline.

Text
Text
Text

'Housegirls Make You Fat' – Joanna Parfitt   Page 1

You can also make a cover page that contains the same information (excluding leader, text and footer of course). This can look very smart. However, again, when you are sending things by email it is not always necessary to go to these lengths. I don't bother to do this at all when I send articles to any of my regular clients.

If you are emailing your article, make sure the pages in your attached document have the same layout as preferred by your destination country. While A4 is standard in the UK and Continental Europe it is not in the US, and this can result in pages printing inaccurately.

Sticking to guidelines

I have said before, and I will say again, that it is vital that you stick to the house style and the guidelines, particularly if you are hoping to be used by the editor for a second time. If the word length required is 750-790 words, then you could probably get away with five to 10 words above or below this, but not much more. If you know your piece is going to be much longer, then ask the editor if this is allowable before you submit it. Sometimes they will decide to make your article a double page spread (DPS) or more.

If you do not have guidelines for the magazine, then write your own. Analyse the magazine and make notes as to article length and style and refer back to them as you write.

Asking questions

An editor would prefer that you asked a couple of questions about your content, interviewees, possible sidebars and length, than that you stayed quiet and hoped for the best. A long letter each time you have a query could get tiresome, but a short, sweet, polite email will be well received.

Sources and surveys

Few editors will fail to ask you for the sources for any statistics or quotes that you use. Make sure that you know where you got your information and add this information to your article. If you quote something from another book or article, then you must credit the original author in full. It is generally acceptable for you to use a sentence or two and give appropriate credits, but use more than that and you will have to get permission from the author or publisher.

Either give the source in the text itself – "According to the 1995 spouse employment survey conducted on behalf of Shell Oil..." – or in the sidebar at the end.

If you want to reproduce a chart, graph or illustration that you have seen elsewhere, again, you will have to get permission and ensure the originator is credited. The editor will expect you to do this. She needs to know that she has permission to use all the material, quotes, illustrations and figures you have provided and that she will have no nasty repercussions from irate interviewees.

Testing it out

It never ceases to amaze me how few people think to read their work out loud to double-check it.

You do not need to have an audience, but it will be quite clear when your sub-clauses are clumsy, or when you have repeated yourself. This is when you identify the 'clunky' writing I mentioned earlier.

It is a good idea to ask someone else to read and comment on your work, but it is not wise to ask someone who is too close to you. My husband is a great critic and tells me the truth about what he thinks. He also makes an effort to be constructive. Some people will not want to offend you and will say nice things even if they don't mean it. Some will not understand your topic and will not dare let on that they feel inadequate. Others may be jealous and so will refuse to give praise where it is due. I believe that it can be valuable to join a writers' circle so that fellow writers can comment. Nevertheless, if there is no one in the group whom you admire, then you could end up receiving useless criticism from people who are less wise than you.

If you want to boost your confidence, test your first pieces on free magazines and papers and see what the reaction is to your work. Then, when you believe in yourself, and, better still, have a few cuttings to prove you have been published, you can move onto bigger and better things.

HOMEWORK ASSIGNMENT SIX

STEP ONE

Write a 650-700 word article (which includes title, leader and sidebars) on one of the topics you gave me at the end of Lesson One or any other topic if you think you have had a better idea since.

- Include some dialogue – use single quotes and British spelling.

- Please explain what illustration you would suggest or provide – one only.

- Please state which publication it is for and the kind of readers this publication attracts.

STEP TWO

Create a new document in Word and use it to submit your assignment.

Name your document with your name, DA (for Definite Articles) and the lesson number. So, if your name is Mary Smith you would name your file MarySmithDA6.

Send this document to your personal tutor by email who will then mark it and send it back to you within two weeks.

Now you can start reading and working with Lesson Seven. However, do not submit the homework for the next Lesson Seven until you have received your critique for Lesson Six.

HOMEWORK SAMPLE SIX

Sam submitted the following homework assignment.

Publication:

Student media, papers or online publications and newsletters targeted at students and recent graduates.

For example, University of London Union's 'London Student', National Union of Students Online, or under the student section of guardian.co.uk.

Article:

Why WWOOF?

Sam Parfitt tells us how he spiced up his long summer holiday with a meaningful get-away on a student budget.

Want to know the best thing about being a student? Summer holidays.

Whilst not all of us are as motivated to hold down a part-time job and spend our well earned break (ahem) building an orphanage in Lesotho or trekking in the Himalayas, there are a multitude of less financially intensive experiences to be had other than spending yet another three months in your pants in front of the television.

World Wide Opportunities on Organic Farms (WWOOF) calls itself 'an international movement that is helping people share more sustainable ways of living' and getting involved provided me with the definite highlight of my longest summer yet.

Essentially a loose network of national organisations and independent hosts, WWOOF links eco-minded people (and even families) with sustainable farms and smallholdings that take on short and long term volunteer workers in exchange for food, accommodation and more of than not, friendship and the experience of an organic lifestyle that so many in today's world would think no longer existed.

I learnt of WWOOF through a friend who had spent the summer previous working on a number of farms in the foothills of the French Pyrenees, and fell in love with the idea of spending some time 'away from it all', experiencing an alternative way of living and clearing my mind of all its accumulated background noise.

My friend also happened to mention that he had met his current girlfriend on one of the farms he had worked at, so there was always that!

There are currently over 75,000 farm hosts in 99 countries worldwide, so the possibilities are endless. Once you have decided where in the world you want to work, the next step is to sign up to the national WWOOF organization, or list of independent hosts, for that area. You will now have access to the contact details of all the registered farms for that country, each with a brief description of the location and function of the farm, as well as what to expect in terms of the type of work you will be doing, who you will be living with, what interests they may have and which languages they speak.

Tamara Hale is an experienced WWOOFer with over ten years of experience under her belt.

'It is always worth spending quite some time deciding which farm to volunteer at,' advises Tamara. 'Although there is something to be said for comfortable accommodation and a convenient location, it will be the experiences of the people you meet and the environment in which you are living and working that will make all the difference,'

'It is also a good idea to contact a few of the farms you like the look of, telling them a little bit about yourself. Say when you would like to work for them as many will be full at the time you ask for. Perhaps the friendly tone of one particular reply will motivate you to want to work there.'

I chose to spend two weeks at *la Ferme d'Art* in Languedoc, France as the owner was fluent in English and encouraged art, music and yoga. He also had a strong focus on sustainability with solar panels, compost toilets and an elaborate system of pools and tanks that collected rainwater and naturally filtered it for drinking and domestic use.

There were two American girls also working on the farm at the same time as me, and we would work together on a variety of jobs from feeding the chickens and harvesting vegetables to painting and repairing fences, from eight in the morning until one. Then, because of the heat we would siesta until six, taking the time to read, hike or sunbathe, before working again until dinner at eight - and in case my joking earlier had got you wondering, unfortunately the both of them had boyfriends already!

Our host, Pan, was a superhero. He was always warm and smiling and it was inspiring to see how he had set up this life for himself. Indeed he had built all the houses himself and rented out one of them to make enough money to give himself the time off to travel. We would always eat and spend our evenings together and Pan would often take us down to the river to swim over siesta, and even to party on Bastille Day!

For me, it was the perfect experience of a lifestyle so peaceful and free. And perhaps best of all, the whole thing cost me only my train ticket down there!

Illustration:

La Ferme d'Art – WWOOFers Caitlin and Waverly, and our host, Pan.

I (Sam Parfitt, 2010) hold the rights to this photograph.

Sidebar:

http://www.wwoof.org/ – a general information site for WWOOF, with links to all recognised national organisations and independent hosts

http://matadornetwork.com/change/a-first-timers-gudie-to-wwoof-ing – 'a first-timers guide to WWOOFing'

http://www.insuchaworld.com/2009/02/08/wwoof-france-follow-up-advice/ – some more good 'how to WWOOF' advice

http://www.guardian.co.uk/travel/2009/may/08/green-ethical-wwoofing-holidays-europe – 'ten of the best WWOOFing breaks in Europe'

http://www.wwoofthemovie.com/ – 'WWOOF The Movie'

LESSON SEVEN

Markets and Marketing

Marketing yourself

The boring bit about being a writer is that no one will ever buy your words if you don't go out there and try to sell them. It takes time before people start to call you with commissions. Here are a few methods to better market yourself:

Enter competitions

One of the best ways to get experience of writing to deadlines, guidelines and length is to enter competitions. The writing magazines run them in every issue. Scour *Writers News, Writers Weekly, Mslexia* and *Writers Forum* for competitions. If you win you will also get published – which means you are growing your cuttings book.

Writing for free

Writing for free is a great way to get going. My first articles were for my university newspaper, and I had the job of reviewing plays and concerts. I often did not understand what I was watching, and so writing for the paper was a good exercise in discipline.

If you want to create a good reputation as a writer, then you need to have your byline appearing in as many publications as possible. If some of this means that you have to write for free, then do consider it. I often write for free, but make sure I keep the copyright for those articles, so that I can sell them for money later, or syndicate them, again, for free. When possible, I make sure that any of my unpaid articles give me a bit of free publicity after my byline, so that readers are able to contact me.

The importance of networking

Networking is a passion of mine. I believe that the people with the most contacts win. In fact, an article in *Readers Digest* stated that the luckiest people are those who know the most people. The more people you know, the more chance you have of receiving an opportunity.

Make friends in every area of your life. Get to know people who know other people in every field and country. And ask them to tell you about any publications they know of. I picked up a copy of *Personnel Today* when at my sister-in-law's house. I then asked her for a back issue and was able to pitch them a story soon after. When at my friend Jenny's, I spotted a copy of a magazine that was for Air Force wives. I borrowed a back issue and was soon writing for them too. Keep your eye out for opportunities at all times – and don't forget to ask!

Not everyone you meet will know of a new market or opportunity for you. Not everyone will be interested in your writing career, but even if some people are never likely to help you, they may well know someone else who could. I call this approach 'clients or cheerleaders'. Make sure that everyone you meet knows what you do. Then they can become your supporter, your referrer, your cheerleader – even if they will never be a client.

Consider the clubs

Find out whether any local clubs have newsletters you could help out with. Find out if they might like you to start one. See if you could write about a local club and send the piece to the business section of your local newspaper. This might not be paid for, but it can be called 'public relations' and that's another string to your bow.

Advertise

Place an advert on a supermarket, health centre, arts centre or office notice board offering your writing services. People often need help with job application letters, mailshots or advertisements. I know writers who have helped people write letters to solicitors or letters of complaint.

Join a writer's circle

Join or start a writers' circle. Members share ideas and markets and there is no reason why you couldn't enter into a joint venture with someone else. I started a writers' circle in every country I have lived. I just put an advert on a supermarket notice board stating that I was looking for people interested in joining a free, informal group. We took it in turns to meet in other people's homes and met once a month. As our members were all very different we learned a lot about the markets in other countries. There is more on writing circles in Lesson Eight.

Go online

Write for online magazines and newsletters, many of which want articles of a quality as high as those required for print publications. Look to see if your favourite websites produce articles and if so, then this is a great market for you. Many websites will offer you nothing more than a byline and a link to your own website or blog as payment. Do not consider writing for the web to be second rate. If anything, owing to the way your online pieces immediately increase your web presence, this kind of writing can be particularly fruitful. Furthermore, whenever you have a piece appear online, you can link to that piece from your own website or blog too.

Write letters

Write letters to the editors of local and international magazines. Find addresses in *The Writers' and Artists' Yearbook* for predominantly UK based publications or *The Writers Market for the USA*. You will also find directories available online for download too.

Find freelance jobs

Subscribe to job opportunities websites. Do a Google search to see if you can find some that specialise in journalism or other writing work. Many of these groups are free to join.

Do a mailshot

Write letters to local companies offering to write for them. In foreign communities companies will often want English-checking prior to publication, mailshots or newsletters.

Other markets

Offer to write for free newspapers or magazines such as school magazines, society newsletters or company magazines. Try to make sure they will print your name or byline. That way you will receive exposure and build your portfolio. Why not offer them book or theatre reviews, or previews of imminent events? Many local interest websites will be delighted to receive this kind of contribution and many may offer you free tickets to events by way of payment.

Book reviews

Book reviews are a great way to get into practice. In general you will get to keep the book you review too. Writing reviews means you will need to get into the habit of getting hold of images of the book covers from the author or publisher and submitting them in the format required by the publication. This is good practice. You will also need to include certain details, such as price and page count, and write to a formula and precise word length. At the end of this program you will find a Bonus Lesson on how to write a book review.

Join the club

Join professional associations that allow you to meet other people who want to work, or do work. Maybe they will have speakers or lectures that will improve your skills? At least you will meet other people who may pass on your name to potential clients. If you join a local business group, for example, you could write a review of each meeting or the publicity for future events. As soon as the members get to know you can write, the opportunities will expand. Grab every opportunity you can to go quote spotting.

Get feedback

Pay for criticism. A 'critique service' or 'manuscript doctor' can be a good start for you and will help you to become more confident in your output. Students of this course are offered six or 12 months of mentoring with critique and leads after they have finished the lessons. Try to find yourself a mentor.

Pitfalls

A career as a writer is not right for everyone. Having worked as an editor as well as a journalist I can see the situations that arise from all angles. Some writers become possessive about their work and hate to see it cut or altered in any way. Unfortunately it is an editor's job to cut and alter work, sometimes asking the writer for more information or quotations several times until she thinks it is right for the publication. If you have been writing about an issue that is very personal to you, you may find it hard to relinquish control like this. An editor's word is always final. Find yourself disagreeing with yours and the chances are you will not be commissioned again. With so many eager writers out there, the editor is rarely in danger of having no writers left to call on!

You may be asked to submit 500 words and then find that the editor cuts your piece by half. This is just the way it goes, I am afraid. Sometimes your piece will be cut and then you will receive a reduced fee accordingly. I was once commissioned to write a piece for a popular women's glossy magazine and duly submitted my 1500 words. The editor wanted me to make changes but I had too many other commitments to be able to do in the time frame. She found a second writer who continued the interviews and spent half a day with me to learn more. When the piece came out the second writer had the byline and I had to fight to receive half of the original fee.

Using the Internet

The Internet is an incredible resource for writers. You can use it to research for articles, to find out which books have been published and to identify suitable people to interview. You can find quotes, statistics and all sorts of useful material. And all for free.
It is generally accepted that as soon as work appears on the Internet it is in the public domain and can therefore be copied by third parties. While you still own the intellectual copyright, it is hard to track who is pinching your work – but equally, you can take ideas from other people. Try to work with integrity and continue to credit any of the authors whose work you use.

It is easy to conduct interviews with people all over the world by email or Skype. Often this can be easier and cheaper than interviewing by phone or in person. However, you tend to get more interesting comments when an interview is conducted live. Remember to print out and keep records of your interviews when possible.

Selling your work

It is important to remember that, as a freelance writer, you will not be writing articles and then trying to sell them. No. You will be having ideas, trying to sell those ideas and *then* writing the articles according to the briefs and guidelines you receive.

The first step towards selling your work is creating an idea that is appropriate to that publication.

The second step is to write a cover letter, or email, most probably to the editor.

Cover letters and outlines

The first contact you will have with an editor will be when you send an outline of your idea. It is common to make this first communication by email.

If you have not been published before, do not say so. Instead prove that you are a specialist in the area you hope to cover in your article.

A cover letter should not exceed one printed page, though of course, if you send an email the length is not so obvious. It is very important that you know the name of the editor. Maybe your piece is for the Features Editor, the Finance Editor or the Health Editor? Check that you spell their name correctly and that you are directing your letter to the right person.

I have been working as a freelancer for many years and have built good relationahips with many editors. In preparation for this course I asked some of them to tell me exactly what encouraged them to use a new, inexperienced writer. Their responses were encouraging, as you will see in the list on the next page.

10 sure-fire ways to make an editor say "yes"

These tips came from my editors at *Stamford Living, Dial, Embrace, Eurograduate* and *American in Britain*.

Tip One

Appear serious about writing. An editor would rather be approached with a handful of good ideas from someone who really wants to be published rather than someone who's just been on holiday and wants to write about their time.

Tip Two

Know the publication (and ideally editor's name!). Round robin communication, or thinking the magazine is consumer when it's customer is a big *faux pas*. Show a genuine interest and understanding in the magazine. Do this and your feature ideas will be perfectly tailored to the readers.

Tip Three

Let the editor feel she can have confidence in you and that your ideas are both good and properly researched. Show that you can write, that you will follow the brief and that you will deliver on time. Most people can string a sentence together – the editor wants evidence that you've got *va-va-voom*. Ideally demonstrate this with how you word your communication, with details of work that's been published or with articles that haven't if you haven't.

Tip Four

Feature-ideas that are topical and that can be backed up with research, surveys and/ or quotes are more useful than a feature that is purely the writer's opinion.

Tip Five

Make the editor believe that once the readers have read the article that they will know something that they didn't know before.

Tip Six

Be prepared to go the extra mile and help a desperate editor with a tight deadline. Help him out, and do it well in double-quick time and you have the chance of becoming a regular writer for the publication. Be confident and say, "sure I can."

Tip Seven

Become an expert in your field and thereby show the editor that you can make a useful contribution to the publication.

Tip Eight

Make the effort to provide good headlines, standfirsts, subheads and resource lists for your articles. Save the editor time.

Tip Nine

Do not pester the editor with weekly emails offering stories. Offer a few great ideas that are perfect for the market every three to six months at most.

Tip Ten

Offer to source photographs for your piece. Maybe you are capable of taking them yourself with a digital camera? If you are writing a piece about someone in another city or country an editor may appreciate a connection with a local photographer.

The perfect pitch

Like I said, you only ever pitch an *idea*. You write the piece upon *commission* and according to the publisher's requirements/brief.

The pitch letter needs to do three things:

1. Present your idea in one or two sentences – this shows it has focus and that you can write without using too many words.

2. Explain why you are the perfect person to write this.

3. Show why your idea is perfect for the publisher/publication.

Here are some examples of good pitch letters:

Example pitch one

Dear Jane

I would like to propose an article for publication in your magazine, *Crafty Cooking*, to which I have subscribed for three years. Provisionally entitled 'Cooks Like it Hot' this 700 word piece would be perfect for your 'Spice it Up' section. Focusing on the use of different, yet widely available red and green chillies, it would explain the appropriate usage of each variety. In my experience, as a South American, who grew up on a capsicum plantation, there is a mystery surrounding the use of chillies in cooking. My article would dispel that myth. After a short introduction about the impact of using fresh, dried or jarred chillies, I would go on to describe 12 different varieties in a glossary format.

I have access to high quality photographs of a wide variety of lesser known chillies, and propose that I provide three South American recipes using them, for your website.

Thank you for your attention. I look forward to hearing from you.

Barbara Pepperdew

Example pitch two

Dear Ms Evans

As a seasoned expatriate wife and mother who has spent more than ten years living overseas in a range of countries I was delighted when *Expatriate Wife* magazine hit the shelves and am now a regular reader.

I would like to propose writing a one page profile of Sarah Brunings for your 'Woman of Our World' section. Sarah has successfully managed to combine running a successful online needlework store with being the parent of triplets and competing in triathlons. She is now based in Brussels, but has also worked in Singapore and New York.

I have already ascertained that Sarah can provide several high quality digital photographs of herself at work, at home and while running. I am sure your readers would be inspired by her story.

My own writing experience has led me to work with several local publications here in Brussels, where I now live and my pieces frequently appear on the *BrusselsOnline* website (you can read a sample at www.brusselsonline.com/xxx).

Thank you for your attention. I look forward to hearing from you.

Yours sincerely

Elena Milopa

Example pitch three

Dear Penny

I was delighted to receive a trial issue of *Entrepreneur* magazine recently. Being an entrepreneur myself, I know firsthand of all the challenges and frustrations that can be encountered. My own business is called Granny's Cakes, and began life in a small farm shop in Dorset.

Marketing on a shoestring has become my specialism and during the eight years I have been in business, I have devised ways to do my marketing without parting with a penny. At the same time, I have watched my business grow at a rate of 25 per cent every year. I would propose writing an article for your 'Real Rural Business' page, in which I would share some of my secrets.

Please could you send me your writers' guidelines so that I might gain a better understanding of *Entrepreneur's* objectives and focus.

Thank you for your attention, I look forward to hearing from you.

Yours sincerely

Jo Parfitt

CVs

If you have a CV or resume that shows evidence of your writing skill and success, then you may attach it to your speculative letters to editors. Some editors like to see them. Others simply do not have time. If you are a new writer then you have nothing to gain by attaching a CV. So I suggest that you wait until you are asked for one, if at all.

If you do produce a 'writing CV', then make sure it fits on one page.

Cuttings

In my experience, very few writers send samples of their previously published work along with their outlines. If you have been published on the Internet, then I suggest that you add the URL of a selection of your work online to the base of your letter. If an editor asks to see samples, then you could send some scans by email attachment, but in my experience this is very rare.

It should be clear from your cover letter whether you can write or not. If you have any spelling or grammar mistakes it will not do you any favours.

Keep copies of every article you have published for your own collection. I used to keep one copy of the whole newspaper or magazine and then a separate copy of the article alone. Over time, I must have collected hundreds of these cuttings and like to look at them and remind myself of my adventures.

If you have your published work together in a file, then it is easy for you to refer back to it, and highly rewarding to watch it grow.

Getting paid

This is a difficult one. In general each magazine or newspaper will have its own rate of pay. This can range from as little as €10 for a short piece to as much as €300-€500 for 1,000 words. Often those magazines with the largest circulation and highest paying advertisers will pay the most. The editor will tell you what pay is on offer, if any. You will not be able to state your own fee, I am afraid.

It is more common to charge by the word than by the page or by the hour. If your article is cut you may be paid according to the final length and not the length of the piece originally submitted.

When you contact a magazine ask for the contributor's guidelines. They will give an indication of the rate of pay to expect as well as the types of pieces and the lengths required.

If you are including illustrations, again, the publication will usually set a fee per picture. They may be used to working with photo libraries or professional photographers, which can be expensive, so they may be rather pleased to find that you can supply quality images for a more reasonable price.

I have often been involved in bartering rather than payment. In general there are so many skilled people available who are not in full-time employment that it is easy to tap into their skills and not pay a penny. I once wrote an article to give publicity to a local potter and he paid me in pots, while the magazine itself paid very poorly. Sometimes bartering can be very advantageous as both sides receive something they want.

Syndication

You are allowed to sell the same piece to more than one magazine. Once the original piece has been published, you can resell your article to print publications and websites in every other country of the world. Some publications stipulate at which point you may resell your piece in their contributor's guidelines or contract.

If you get commissioned by a publication that wants to retain the copyright for your piece, so that you cannot resell it, you will be asked to sign a contract. No contract? The piece will be yours to resell as often as you can.

Syndication is a great way to increase your web presence and I do this a lot. However, I always try to tweak a previously published piece so that it is honed for the new market and very often alter the opening paragraph and the titles so that it is less obvious that it appeared somewhere else before.

HOMEWORK ASSIGNMENT SEVEN

STEP ONE

Write a cover letter to your target publication, proposing that you write the article which you submitted as homework after Lesson Six. If you don't already know the name of the relevant editor – find out!

STEP TWO

Create a new document in Word and use it to submit your assignment.

Name your document with your name, DA (for Definite Articles) and the lesson number. So, if your name is Mary Smith you would name your file MarySmithDA7.

Send this document to your personal tutor by email who will then mark it and send it back to you within two weeks.

Now you can start reading and working with Lesson Eight. However, do not submit the homework for the next Lesson Eight until you have received your critique for Lesson Seven.

HOMEWORK SAMPLE SEVEN

Erin submitted the following homework sample.

Cover letter:

Mike Deme, Editor
Adventure Cycling
mdeme@adventurecycling.org
406-721-1776 x 222

Dear Mr Deme

When I tell people I am a cyclist living in the Netherlands, I always get the same response, "Perfect! There are tons of cyclist there, you must love it." Ugh, if only it were that simple.

Any expat will tell you that the first year in a new country is much lonelier than one's initial expectations. Living out of your comfort zone is a daily, if not hourly occurrence in a foreign land. After many months of trying to find my way, hope appeared in an unlikely place – peddling my beloved bicycle up the magnificent Italian Alps with 10,000 other cyclists from all over the world.

I would like to write an 1100 word essay for your 'The Final Mile' section of *Adventure Cyclist*. The narrative would tell of my move from cycling Mecca Boulder, Colorado, to the commuter-crazed country of Holland and finally, the ride of a lifetime at the Maratona dles Dolomites. The story would include humorous encounters with an Italian, a German and a group of Columbians, all proving what cyclists already know – that bonds form quickly amongst fellow peddlers.

I can provide 300-dpi photos of the ride at your request. Additionally, if you have room for a side bar, I will happily include factual information about the Maratona dles Dolomites including ride length, location, number of participants, dates, and so on. This piece may also provide an advertising opportunity with the Maratona dles Domomites event, as they are looking to increase participation with North American riders.

If you would like to commission me to write this please let me know your deadline. I appreciate your time and look forward to hearing back from you.

Sincerely

Erin X

Freelance writer

LESSON EIGHT

Making it happen

In this lesson I'm going to talk about all the things that can get in the way of your writing dreams. The things that block you, make you procrastinate and lead, disappointingly, to the demise of that dream. I want you to succeed as a freelance writer. That's why I plan to unpick every myth that may try to block your ascent to publishing heaven. Let's start...

Dealing with rejection

How we all hate to be rejected. There are many reasons for rejection and most of them will have nothing to do with your writing ability. Maybe your article is not quite right for the publication? Maybe they have already commissioned a feature on a similar subject? Maybe they have just accepted a piece on the same topic from an inferior writer, but are unwilling to go back on their decision? Maybe the magazine is going through difficulties and they have no budget for freelancers? Maybe the magazine uses staff writers for features and rarely uses a freelancer? Maybe you offer them a travel column, but they like to use the same travel journalist every issue, so there is no opportunity for a new writer in that slot? Maybe your idea is unlikely to attract a related advertisement and they need to sell the opposite page at full price?

The sad thing is that editors are so busy that they may not have time to reply to your speculative letter at all, or they may only have time to offer you a short, curt reply.

Try not to become downhearted. And most importantly, try not to take rejection personally. When I was editor of *Woman Abroad*, we used about 30 articles in each issue. We published bi-monthly, so we had opportunities for 180 articles a year. I had my favourite writers of course, and those I used each issue, but I tried hard to use anyone with talent once, so that I could give everyone a chance. All the same, I must have heard from 20 to 40 writers a month and, while I made a point of replying as fully as possible to everyone, it was impossible to use every good idea that came my way.

We used to have a theme for each issue too. Sometimes the theme was repatriation, or third culture kids, or the expatriate marriage. That meant that if someone sent me a piece on a theme related to one of our special focuses, and that focus was pencilled in for a year's time, I had to make them wait months for a final answer.

Put yourself in the shoes of the editor and try to understand the reasons why she has to say no.

And remember – even if you are rejected outright, you can contact the magazine in a year's time to see if things have changed. When there is a new editor or a change of publisher all kinds of things can change.

The irony is that if you are rejected, you will have been rejected on the strength, not of your article and journalism skills, but your cover letter. This is why it is so important to get your initial communication right.

How not to be a nuisance

Editors are busy. I've been one, and I've worked with many. There are tight deadlines and tight budgets. Sometimes time is so tight that they make the wrong decision, and your piece would have been 100 times better than the one they used. If you have not heard back from an editor about your proposal within a month, then I think it is fair to contact them again, very briefly, to check that they received your letter. If you still don't hear anything, then try again another month later.

If you still hear nothing, then you could write again and ask what kind of pieces they are looking for. Try not to nag and badger the editor. It will usually make her cross.

If a magazine is monthly, then the week or so directly prior to printing is hectic. An editor is unlikely to find time to look through proposals until that issue is well and truly 'put to bed'. Giving an editor a month to reply is fair. If she is interested, she will get back in touch.

Lateral thinking

It is a good idea to spread your net as wide as possible. So you could either try to pitch the same story to a range of markets or pitch a range of stories to one market. Or, of course, you could do both.

Nothing focuses the mind more effectively than the promise of money, though, I find. And if a publication uses my work I will make myself aware of their editorial calendar (how often they commission) and pitch them something else once the first article has been published. Find out what kind of pieces interest them most and make it your business to do some research in those areas.

The reality is that things change. You have to keep permanently on your toes. You need to continually have new ideas, find new publications and think laterally.

Over the years I have written for countless publications, approached many more and been rejected, or ignored by more still. After two years doing a column for *Resident Abroad,* the magazine changed ownership, changed name and decided to dispense with my services. After 18 months writing for the 'Smart Moves' section of *The Independent on Sunday,* the section editor moved on, and the section was closed down. After a year of writing almost all the content for the 'Expat Living' page for the *Weekly Telegraph,* they decided to start using a range of journalists (fortunately they took me back on an even better deal two years later). I wrote for *Emirates Woman* for five years, but when I moved to Oman, they never used me again.

This is how it is. Each of these publications provided me with a regular income and losing it was hard to handle. But magazines change staff and close sections. In fact, I have worked for two publications that went bankrupt. It can be hard to bounce back again and again. But that is what life is like when you work freelance. It is dangerous to put all your eggs in one basket, or to write for a limited number of publications. That is why it is so important to keep looking for new markets and ideas. But more importantly, you have to keep approaching them too.

Regardless of the amount of success you are having in your preferred field you must keep looking for new ones.

A systematic approach

I suggest that you give yourself a list of tasks to accomplish that are manageable. Take your list of publications and article ideas and promise yourself that you will contact one publication and pitch one story every week, for example. At the same time, you will approach one of the more poorly paid markets each week or month too. And meanwhile, you will network and attend a writers' circle. Set some monthly goals, such as the example, below:

Monthly goals

- Pitch four stories per month to four new publications (two unpaid, one local, one international).

- Pitch two stories per month to previously contacted publications.

- Spend one hour per month surfing the Net to find new publications and websites.

- Spend one hour per month reading free writing market e-zines.

- Read one writing book or magazine per month.

- Attend a writers' circle for one evening a month.

- Attend an interesting event or meeting once a month to get ideas and inspiration, go quote spotting and meet new people.

- Contact every publication you have ever approached once a year, even if they rejected you, to see if things have changed.

If this is too much for you, trim it down. Promise yourself that you will pitch one story a month, or whatever, but stick to it. The more you send out there, the more chance you have of success.

Believe in yourself

The best way to sell your writing services effectively is to believe in yourself. If you are passionate about what you do, and about your subjects, then this passion will manifest itself as enthusiasm, and enthusiasm is infectious. If you don't believe in yourself you can't expect someone else to either.

I believe that the best way to develop self-belief is to get published. And the easiest way to ensure success is to write, at first for publications that don't pay. Even if they don't pay they'll still only use work that fits their brief, meets their deadline and is the right word count, so getting accepted by an editor, any editor, is always something to be proud of.

If you are having trouble believing in yourself enough to cold call editors or send unsolicited emails to them, then ask your friends for a referral. Someone is bound to know an editor, agent, publisher, writing tutor or journalist. Just ask that person, using your friend's referral, if they would mind giving you 15 minutes on the phone as a kind of mentor, just to help you realise you are on track. Or ask if that person would mind giving one of your completed articles the once-over, and to tell you what they think, honestly.

The endorsement of someone you regard as a role model will do wonders for your self-esteem.

Nothing gives you more self-belief than a paycheck for your writing. I have written CVs for a living, and computer manuals, even the brochure for an architect. See if you can get some kind of paid writing work, even if not in your chosen field. Then you will believe you can write.

The value of the 'Shitty First Draft'

In her great book, *Bird by Bird*, Ann Lamott, talks of the value of what she calls 'the Shitty First Draft'. Let me explain:

Many new writers try to be perfect. As a result they become hypercritical and rarely reach the end of an article because they get stuck on a less than wonderful opening paragraph. Lamott and I are firm believers in getting it written, however imperfectly, and getting to the end. It is easier to go back and polish a finished, rushed piece of writing, than it is to reach the end of a piece, polishing as you go.

One of the reasons I endorse this belief is because I recognise that getting started is very difficult. Sometimes you can't seem to set the scene, or introduce the topic accurately and so give up early. I find that my opening paragraphs are often under par too. But I also find that once I have reached the end I then go back and write the introduction last. By then I did know what I was going to write about and could write a better introduction as a result.

If you give yourself permission to just write it, gaps, mistakes and all, but to get to the end, you may find, like me, like Lamott, that reaching a 'Shitty First Draft' is quite an achievement, and that the polishing is then a piece of cake. Try it.

Subscribe to a writing magazine

You will need to face a constant stream of ideas for articles that have seen publication, to learn of new markets and to give yourself more practice by entering competitions. Magazines, both on and offline, will also inspire you with success stories and case studies, interviews with popular writers and information about courses you could attend.

Writers News is published in England but there are other such magazines published in other countries.

Join or start a Writers' Circle

Local writers' circles tend to advertise in international club newsletters, school newsletters or at arts centres. If you cannot locate one in your area then start one.

Advertise that you are looking for people to join an informal writer's circle that will meet in members' homes. I find that fortnightly meetings from 8-10 pm work best. As soon as you have two other recruits hold a meeting.

At the meeting

1. Start by introducing yourselves, saying why you joined the circle, what you hope to get out of it and what you can offer the group. Bring along any tips, publications you'd recommend, and any recent work you may have had published.

2. If anyone has brought along a piece they have been working on then invite her to read it aloud. Alternatively, ensure copies have been made and that you can all read it yourselves. Discuss the pieces, giving any opinions – even if they are critical.

3. Share any relevant information, competitions, markets or news you may have gleaned since the last meeting.

4. Set a task to complete during the meeting. Often a timed writing exercise can be effective. Ask a member to think of a subject, say, 'why I write' or 'parents' or 'I remember' and then start to write for ten minutes without erasing or lifting the pen from the paper. If you get stuck then keep on writing the title over and over until inspiration comes. It is amazing how deep this experience makes you go into your subconscious and what stories it provokes.

5. Set a task for completion for the next meeting.

Often writers' circles invite guest speakers, editors, writers and so on. Some will be prepared to come for free as long as they can sell their own books. Others will want expenses only.

It can work quite well if you ask the person who is hosting the meeting to think up a potential task and homework. Try to ensure that projects are balanced between fiction, non-fiction, poetry and exercises. If all members of the group hate poetry then don't do it!

Why not consider collating completed and approved work into an annual anthology? This can be a good souvenir of the year, but also provides another way of getting into print and earning some money.

Some highly successful circles are run on a much more formal basis. Members provide printed copies of their pieces in advance and criticism is more thorough.

I find that an informal approach works well if your objective is to encourage people to write and not feel bad if they have not produced any work.

Although I like to meet fortnightly, some circles I know have speakers once a fortnight and a manuscript evening once a fortnight too. See what works for you.

Join or start a Reading Circle or Book Club

If you want to be inspired then you need to open your mind to different styles of writing. Discussing published books with other people, whether they are classics, prizewinners, or self-published novels, will increase your knowledge and help you to be more discerning. It will also give you ideas for your own style and plots and what may be possible.

Read

If you want to write articles, read articles. If you want to write novels, read novels. Feed your mind with inspiration and ideas by reading what you want to write about. But also consider reading books such as *The Artist's Way* by Julia Cameron or *Writing Down the Bones* by Natalie Goldberg because they will help you to feel you are a writer and that you are living your dream. Read *Chicken Soup for the Writer's Soul* or other writers' soul food.

Make time for inspiration

You cannot hope to be inspired and have ideas if you do not give yourself the time to think. Time to be on your own. Try turning off the car radio when you are driving, go for walks or sit in the sun. Make a space in your mind for your ideas.
Now, feed your soul further by spending time with people who inspire you. Put yourself in a position where you can exchange ideas and talk about what matters to you. A writers' circle is a good place, of course, but you can also give yourself permission to have lunch, coffee or days out with people who energise you.

Keep a notepad and pen with you at all times so that you can write down your ideas when they come to you.

Get into print – any way you can

This could indeed be the hardest part of all; after all it is the reason you took this course. Honestly though, getting published isn't really the problem. It's being paid for it that is harder! Again, I am going to suggest you write for free at first.

Everyone has to start somewhere. So, offer to write something for the school newsletter, report on the parents' association, or a thrift sale. Share information about a great day out you enjoyed recently. Often local papers will pay for information about what's on and what's been on in your town or village. In 2005 my local paper paid 5p a word.

Send in reports about local events to your local newspaper or magazine. They will probably consider using your piece if it is well written and relevant. They may even pay you for it.

If you see an advertisement that has been badly written, and you feel you can improve it, write your improved copy and send it to the advertiser free of charge. They may commission you to work for them next time round. Then again they may ignore you – but it is worth a try.

Offer to produce any advertisements or editorial for school or club magazines.

Find a friend who has a new business or product and ask if you can write them a press release. Send it out to appropriate publications – find them in one of the press guides I have told you about, or which are mentioned in the 'Resources' section.

Be flexible. Writing is just words. Think of any way you can to put words on paper and then see them reproduced. Why not write recipes, itineraries, brochures, curriculum vitae, mailshots, letters to the Editor, your Christmas letter? Write anything. Sooner or later someone will pay you for something. Then you will have the confidence in yourself and a real portfolio.

Being original

Don't go thinking that there are no original ideas and that it has all been done before, and so there is no hope for you. Sure, it has been said that there are only 35 potential short story plots in the world. Do not be disheartened by such a statement. Any story can be rewritten with a new character, a new setting or a new angle. Someone else may have written a similar piece, but that writer wasn't you. That writer did not have your experience, your style, your contacts or your resources. Your version will be different.

As a new writer there are countless reasons for sticking with small, local publishers at first. Chances are local publishers will not receive piles of mail from young hopefuls every day, unlike their national giant-sized counterparts. Chances are they may welcome new writers too, even if they are likely to pay less. If you are in a transient expatriate community you are in an even better position, for publishers will need a constant supply of freelancers. A newcomer to the community will have fresh ideas and new eyes. Often this is just what an editor needs, and she will give you the opportunity that you need.

Once you have cut your teeth on local publications you can start branching out to the rest of the world. If you have been living in Malaysia for any length of time, you are an expert. Think of all the magazines outside the country who may want to know about it. Travel, in-flight, colour supplements, crafts magazines, company newsletters, business, camping, diving, driving — the list is endless. Okay, so you may have read articles on Norway in the colour supplements and magazines, but have you read about camping in Norway in a camping magazine, or candle making in a craft magazine? Maybe you could research the railways, Viking history, or the fish industry, and sell such pieces to specialist magazines? There is always a new angle out there.

Writing is fast becoming one of the most popular careers. Getting into print really isn't that hard if you remember to consider smaller, local and even free publications first. Let's recap on some of the ideas I have shared with you in this course and put them in the order that you should consider doing them.

Your route to success

Below is a reminder of the route I recommend you take towards success and profit:

1. Create an ideas book in which you jot down all your ideas as they come to you and contact details of interesting people or resources you could use some day.

2. Create a list of submissions, when and where you pitch pieces and the results you get.

3. Start a blog, choose a theme or focus you can sustain and pledge to write at least once a week.

4. Join Twitter and pledge to tweet about all your articles and blog posts as they occur.

5. Write reviews for websites and local print and online publications – book reviews, theatre reviews and event reviews are easiest. Link to those pieces on your blog and tweet about the blog posts. Continue to do this for every piece that you have published. Some local publications will be happy to pay you a fee. Ensure all pieces include your author bio and a link to your blog.

6. Collect print publications everywhere you go and that could provide you with potential markets. Take a look at their contributor's guidelines.

7. Write short features on topics of local interest to club and free magazines and websites.

8. Write articles on your area of interest, including interviews and with reference to good resources, based on your knowledge, and to books and websites you can include in sidebars. Write these for websites and free local publications that are interested in these topic areas.

9. Start pitching to print publications that focus on your own areas of interest or expertise. Some of these may offer a fee.

10. Start pitching to airline magazines and member/subscriber/company magazines. All of these are likely to offer a fee.

11. Start pitching to any publications on and offline for which you have great, new ideas and that will pay you for your pieces. And if they don't have a budget to pay you, see if you can syndicate or rework existing articles there. Always insist on having a bio with link to your blog if there is no fee available.

12. Build a portfolio of all your published work.

Getting ideas

The following ideas have been included here to help maintain a steady stream of creativity.

Write a list of all the types of article you feel you could write about, such as:

- Divorce in your sixties
- Window box gardening
- 10 tips to make marriage survive
- Portable careers
- Vietnam off the beaten track
- Where to get the perfect cup of coffee
- Visitors and how to handle them
- Doing business abroad
- Surviving Malaria

_____

_____

_____

_____

_____

_____

_____

_____

_____

_____

_____

_____

_____

_____

_____

_____

_____

_____

Now write a list of all the publications you know of, and would like to analyse with a view to pitching a story, such as:

- *Readers Digest*
- *Woman's Own*
- *Vietnam Today*
- *Trout and Salmon Fishing*
- *American Wives Club Magazine*
- *Sainsbury's Magazine*
- *Living Abroad*
- *Gulf Air*

_____

_____

_____

_____

_____

_____

_____

_____

_____

_____

_____

_____

_____

_____

_____

Now write the name of each publication on a separate piece of paper and list the specific articles you could write for each.

Right now you may only have two or three ideas, but over time you will have more.

Page one
Readers Digest
Marriage on the Move
Surviving Malaria

Page two
Talesmag.com
Living in Vietnam
Surviving the in-laws' month long visits

Page three
Vietnam Today
Marriage guidance in Vietnam

International schools in Vietnam

Put these 'publication-headed sheets' into a ring bound file, and put some spare sheets in the back so that you can add new publications as you come across them.

Promise yourself that you will find the names of the relevant section editors for each publication and approach them with a first story.

Write the date of your first communication alongside each article and then leave space for the date you received a reply and its outcome.

Keep your eye out for new publications, new stories and new interviewees. Write them down and add them to your file regularly.

If you seem to be getting nowhere with one publication, or one topic idea, then try another. If you seem to be drawing a blank with paid publications, then approach some publications that don't pay and build up your clippings and your confidence.

Free writing

Find yourself a quiet spot and make yourself speedwrite for ten minutes on one of the following topics:

- I remember
- When I grow up
- Home
- In an ideal world
- I know
- I love
- If only
- I dream of
- Planes
- If I had a day to myself
- Old friends
- Driving
- Exercise

Now look back at what you have written and see how many article ideas come into your mind.

Start with a title

Sometimes your starting point for a new article will be the title. If a great idea for a title pops into you head, take that title and think up all the different ways you could write a piece based on that title.

Choose one of the following titles I have made up and try to think of five different types of articles you could write for each. For example, if I gave you the title *Broads Abroad* you could write about:

- Prostitution abroad
- Obesity in expatriate children
- Female friendship overseas
- American women on holiday
- Activities for single women overseas on business

Now it's your turn

Your titles are:

Driving me mad

Idea 1 _____

Idea 2 _____

Idea 3 _____

Idea 4 _____

Idea 5 _____

Just deserts

Idea 1 _____

Idea 2 _____

Idea 3 _____

Idea 4 _____

Idea 5 _____

All part of the service

Idea 1 _____

Idea 2 _____

Idea 3 _____

Idea 4 _____

Idea 5 _____

You've got a friend

Idea 1 _____

Idea 2 _____

Idea 3 _____

Idea 4 _____

Idea 5 _____

Outsiders

Idea 1 _____

Idea 2 _____

Idea 3 _____

Idea 4 _____

Idea 5 _____

Moving story

Idea 1 _____

Idea 2 _____

Idea 3 _____

Idea 4 _____

Idea 5 _____

Start with an existing article

Now let's really get those idea muscles working.

Find a publication that you would like to write for some day. Now pick an article from that publication that you particularly like. Consider five ways you could alter that idea for the same market and five more ways that you could adjust it for a different market. For example, in a parenting magazine you may see a piece on communicating with teenagers. How might this inspire you? Here are my ideas:

Five ideas for the same market could be:

1. Communicating with expat teenagers
2. Communicating with step-teenagers
3. Communicating with toddlers
4. Communicating with children from a blended family
5. Communicating with children after a divorce

Five ideas for different markets could be:

1. Yachting magazine – communicating with teenagers in a confined space
2. Expat magazines – telling teenagers about an imminent new posting
3. Property magazines – how to make your teenagers feel involved in your house renovation project
4. Education magazine – how parent-teachers can communicate with their own children inside school
5. Food magazine – how to get your teens interested in doing their own cooking, in preparation for university

Start with a publication

Imagine you have an idea for a story about a 70-year-old man who decided to emigrate to Spain from Britain with his six cats and live on the beach in the Costa del Sol. Try to think of six publications who might like to take a story based on this connection and how you might need to adjust the story to fit each of them. I'll start you off:

1. A pet lovers' magazine, which takes pieces on pet lovers that do unusual things.

2.

3.

4.

5.

6.

Start with an inspiring person

Think of all the people you have met during your life or on your travels. Choose ten of them and write their names here. Now think about what they have done, what they know and what makes them interesting. Think of at least two stories you could write about each of them.

Person 1:

      Idea 1 _____

      Idea 2 _____

Person 2:

      Idea 1 _____

      Idea 2 _____

Person 3:

    Idea 1 _____

    Idea 2 _____

Person 4:

    Idea 1 _____

    Idea 2 _____

Person 5:

    Idea 1 _____

    Idea 2 _____

Person 6:

    Idea 1 _____

    Idea 2 _____

Person 7:

    Idea 1 _____

    Idea 2 _____

Person 8:

    Idea 1 _____

    Idea 2 _____

Person 9:

    Idea 1 _____

    Idea 2 _____

Person 10:

    Idea 1 _____

    Idea 2 _____

Start with an expert

Make a list of six people you know who you consider to be an expert about something. They might include a professional water skier, a mother of twins or someone who has moved country ten times or learned five languages, for example. All articles benefit from having some quotes from experts. Make a list of your experts now, and think of the types of article they could be useful for. I'll start you off:

Expert 1: Jenny Martin, website designer

    Idea 1 <u>ten things not to do when designing a website</u>

    Idea 2 <u>is website designing a good portable career?</u>

Expert 2:

    Idea 1 _____

    Idea 2 _____

Expert 3:

    Idea 1 _____

    Idea 2 _____

Expert 4:

    Idea 1 _____

    Idea 2 _____

Expert 5:

    Idea 1 _____

    Idea 2 _____

Expert 6:

    Idea 1 _____

    Idea 2 _____

The waiting game

Probably the hardest part of all is the waiting. Waiting for your tutor's response to your last assignment. Waiting for the writers' circles' reaction to your recent poem. Waiting to hear from all those publishers you contacted. It can be tough. Busy publishers can take up to three months to reply. Local magazines tend to work much faster. Then, they usually want your piece immediately. Publishers can never wait.

You submit your piece. You feel excited already. You forget about it. Three months later they call to say your piece will appear in an issue eight months away. You will be paid upon publication of course. So now you have to contain your excitement and wait to see yourself in print. Then you have to wait at least another month for the money.

In the meantime keep on writing, having ideas, filling the well, reading your books and magazines, writing letters to editors, attending courses and maintaining your enthusiasm.

Be patient, keep track of what you have sent and to where. See where you are having most success. Keep on with all the steps above and you will get there in the end.

HOMEWORK ASSIGNMENT EIGHT

By now you should really feel like a writer.

STEP ONE

Your final task is to write a complete article of your choice for your tutor to critique. State which publication you have in mind for it, and before you send it off, please check that you have adhered to that publication's guidelines.

STEP TWO

Create a new document in Word and use it to submit your assignment.

Name your document with your name, DA (for Definite Articles) and the lesson number. So, if your name is Mary Smith you would name your file MarySmithDA8.

Send this document to your personal tutor by email who will then mark it and send it back to you within two weeks.

Please do not submit the homework for Lesson Eight until you have received my critique for Lesson Seven.

HOMEWORK SAMPLE EIGHT

Erin submitted the following homework assignment.

Target publication:

Online magazine for an airline that flies to any airport that is close to the race.

Article:

Amongst Friends

Struggling to find her way as a new expat in the Netherlands, writer and avid sports woman finds refuge and comfort in an unlikely place; The Maratona dles Dolomites, one of the most gruelng bicycling events in Europe.

I thought moving from Boulder, Colorado to the Netherlands would be a seamless transition from one big cycling community to another. I'd join a women's club, meet tons of friends and be a happy expat. What I came to realize some months into the move was that not all bike communities are created equally.

I hail from a sports enthusiasts' Mecca where recreational cyclists line roads for fitness and fun. Coffee shops play Tour de France race video on the big screen and people discuss optimal color combinations for their cars and rough racks. No one flinches at smooth legged men in skin-tight 'costumes' and clicky medal shoes.

And while the population of bikes is triple that of its inhabitants in Holland, getting to work is the ultimate goal, not getting up Flagstaff Mountain. When I tell Dutch people I ride a road bike they seem confused.

'You mean a race bike? You race your bike like Lance?'

'Well yes, but no. I don't race,' I say, which is where I usually lose them. Most of the road cyclists here have gray hair, if any, and are male. Or they ride with Lance. And while I love the sight of an impeccably dressed Dutch woman cruising through town on a rickety old townie with three small kids hanging from all sides, it's just not quite what I had pictured as my cycling community.

After three months of listening to me complain of loneliness and identity loss in my new life abroad, my boyfriend made me an offer he knew I wouldn't refuse.

'We're signed up for the Maratona. The hotel is booked, meals are arranged, and our schedules are clear,' he said.

'You're kidding!' I jumped out of my chair so quickly it would have given Mark Cavendish a startle.

The Maratona dles Dolomites is the most celebrated granfondo bicycle ride in the world. The event attracts 10,000 cyclists from forty-five countries and covers seven mountain passes through the Italian Alps.

Initially I was a bit nervous. I hadn't clocked too many miles in the past six months thanks to the distraction of an international move. And, as a new lowlander, I had surely de-acclimated to altitude riding. But we pulled into the charming ski town of Corvara, and the doubt was quickly replaced by excitement. I gawked out the window at the colossal mountain peaks bursting with anticipation. Cyclists everywhere bustled around in their logo-clad Lycra. Lines of shiny road bikes leaned against terraces and cafes for miles. Famed cyclist Mario Cipollini posed for photos with fans in the street ten feet from me. I yearn to be on my bike.

Wahoo! There, look, finally cyclists like me. It was like coming home. For the first time since arriving in Europe, I was within my comfort zone.

Adrenaline pulsed through me on the morning of the ride. A slight chill filled the early morning air. I made my way to the starting line, filing tightly into place with thousands of other cyclists. The sun peaked over the mountains. Two helicopters swirled above our heads with cameramen dangling out. An announcer's voice boomed impassioned cheers in Italian over the loudspeaker. Men and women hurried behind bushes to empty their bladders one last time.

I scanned the crowd, reading names and countries listed on the race numbers pinned to everyone's backs. Mostly Italians, but at least fifteen other nationalities were within reach, gathered here together with one goal in mind. We were strangers each with our own sets of language barriers and cultural differences, but the energy in the air was clear, I was amongst friends. Our unspoken bond was our passion for cycling.

I rode that day with a giant smile plastered across my face. I pushed myself to go faster, to pass as many people as possible. I was swept up in the excitement of it all. Spectators hollered along course.

'Brava, Brava! Great job, almost done!' Only later that evening would my aching muscles remind me how under-trained I really was.

On the final pass, the Falzarego, I found myself battling up the 2105 meter climb with a middle-aged Italian named Alessandro. It was obvious by that point that Italian men did not appreciate a woman passing them by. Alessandro and I yoyo-ed back and forth for miles, I passed him with a burst of energy, only to quickly be overtaken again. It went on and on. Upon sighting what I thought was the final peak, I crept up behind him until just the right moment – and then putting in a final effort, I surged just as we crested the hill. He casually rode by me, smirking, as I gasped for air in triumph.

'Di nuovo?' he nodded in the direction of the actual final climb, a 300-meter wall straight up into space. I laughed with wide eyes, shaking my head.

'No no, I'm done,' I said.

I rolled across the finish line about an hour later, the sun blazing overhead. Celebration and stories filled the rest of the day and evening. The next morning we packed our dirty bikes and tired legs into the car and headed north. Nine hours later, the sun moved out and the rain drizzled down around us. The landscape flattened out around me and we were home again in the Netherlands. I was still an outsider, a foreigner, but always a cyclist.

Sidebar:

If you go...

- Book early! The ride is so popular registration is done by lottery. Pre-registration is Oct. 14th - Nov. 4th. More info: http://www.maratona.it/info/how-to-register/en

- Train, train, and then train some more. The Maratona is a timed event and while the roads are closed to cars during the event forcing officials to enforce a maximum time limit for each event.

- Chose your distance wisely. The event offers three distances, all covering breathtaking yet punishing terrain:

Maratona dles Dolomites course
Lenght: 138 km
Difference in height: 4190 m

Middle course
Length: 106 km
Difference in height: 3090 m

Sellaronda course
Lenght: 55 km
Difference in height: 1780 m

- Prepare for the masses. The Maratona is an extremely organized, well-run event. However with **8,798** participants from 42 countries at the start, you will need to pay attention to avoid any minor disasters.

Now, you are on your own

Or are you? If you would like to be mentored, guided and to receive feedback on your articles and pitch letters then maybe you should consider signing up for my six months' mentoring scheme? Details are at the fron of this workbook.

If, like many students who have taken this program, you now feel confident enough to break into the world of the freelance writer for real, then I wish you lots of luck and thank you for sharing this journey with me.

With very best wishes

Happy writing

Jo Parfitt

Resources

There are many websites bursting with free information. Lots of them will give you free e-books or free newsletters. Here are just a few:

Books

Writing From Life
By Susan Wittig Albert
Published by Tarcher Puttnam

How to Write and Sell a Synopsis
By Stella Whitelaw
Published by Allison and Busby

Successful Syndication
By Michael Sedge
Published by Allworth Press

An Author's Guide to Publishing
Michael Legat
Hale

Writing for Pleasure and Profit
Michael Legat
Hale

The Writer's Companion
Barry Turner
Macmillan

Becoming a Writer
Dorothea Brande
Macmillan

Literary Agents: What They Do, How They Do It, and How to Find and Work with the Right One for You, Revised and Expanded
Michael Larsen
Wiley

Writers' and Artists' Yearbook
http://www.writersandartists.co.uk/
A&C Black

Writing Personal Essays: How to Shape Your Life Experiences for the Page
Sheila Bender
Writers Digest Books

Get Yourself Published
Suzan St Maur
Lean Marketing Press

Websites

Freelance Writing
http://www.freelancewriting.com/

Writing World
www.writing-world.com

Absolute Write
www.absolutewrite.com

Writers Weekly
www.writersweekly.com

SPANnet
www.spannet.org

Writers Digest
www.writersdigest.com

Author Link
www.authorlink.com

The Well-Fed Writer
www.wellfedwriter.com

Writer Gazette
www.writergazette.com

Aspire2Write
www.aspire2write.com

All You Can Read
www.allyoucanread.com

Journalism Net
www.journalismnet.com

Jobs

Jobs 4 Journalists
www.jobs4journalists.co.uk

Electronic newsletter subscriptions

Your EveryDay Write
YourEveryDayWrite@yahoogroups.com

Work For Writers
WorkForWriters@yahoogroups.com

The Write Choice
TheWriteChoice@yahoogroups.com

Find freelance markets, grants, and competitions:
http://www.fundsforwriters.com

BONUS ONE

How to write a book review

Writing a book review is a great way to get your name in print. It is also a way to get yourself a free book.

Authors and publishers need their books to be reviewed in as many places as possible. It provides vital publicity.

What can you write about?

It can be useful to specialise in one or two areas. In this way you can build a database of websites, magazines, newspapers, trade publications, free publications and so on that also focus on your area. Publications like to print reviews, not least because they are good space fillers, but also because they can be easily illustrated with the book's cover.

Sometimes the book's publisher will offer a special discount or free copies to readers too, which makes the publication even happier to take the review. Furthermore, if they do not have to pay for your review they will be even happier still.

I specialise in writing reviews of books that are of interest to people living and working abroad or in the publishing industry, like myself, and that means that I regularly receive the latest editions of books on subjects such as:

- Buying property abroad
- Living and working in certain countries
- People who live or work or travel overseas
- Novels with an expat theme
- Self-development
- Careers
- Portable careers
- Expatriate careers
- General books by an expatriate author
- Changing your life
- Getting published
- Writing
- Self-publishing

And many more...

Where can you source the books to review?

Because of my own specialist areas, I regularly receive books from:

- Culture Smart!
- Kogan-Page
- Nicholas Brealey International
- Howtobooks
- Times Warner
- Survival Books
- Lean Marketing Press
- Expatriate Press
- Capstone
- Seal Press
- John Wiley
- Summertime Publishing

And countless small presses, as well as the authors themselves. Keep your eyes open for new publications. As the owner of Summertime Publishing, I also publish books by and for expats regularly, so you can always ask me for review copies too.

In the first instance contact the publishers and ask them to send you press releases for new books. Then, once you have a guarantee that a popular website or publication will take your reviews, you can ask for a copy of the book to be posted to you, or to receive a PDF version via email. So long as the publication you are writing for is read by potential purchasers of the book you hope to review, most publishers will be happy to send you a book. And yes, you do get to keep it!

So, how do you review a book?

Check the target publication for any existing reviews and you will get an idea of how many words they are as well as the kind of information they include. For example, the review **may** contain the following information before the text of your review:

- ISBN number
- Author name
- Book title
- Book subtitle
- Publisher
- Website of publisher
- Number of pages
- Type of book – hardback/paperback for example
- Price

- Publication date
- Edition number

If you have no sample review to model before you write yours then ask the editor of the website/magazine/paper what they need you to include. Ask too how many words they want, and then ensure you write to that length. Typically, reviews are short at between 100 and 300 words. The word count includes the factual information at the start. Do not forget to put your own name, your byline, at the end of the piece.

Six steps to writing a book review

1. Identify a book you would like to review.

2. Find a publication that will agree to take your review and find out:

   a. Their required word count
   b. The information you need to include
   c. When they want the review by
   d. Whether they want a cover illustration and of what size and format
   e. Request your press copy of the book and any existing press releases and cover illustration
   f. Receive the book
   g. Read the back cover text, the flyleaf and any accompanying press release you may have been sent. Often, it is convenient to paraphrase some of this for your review. After all, the publisher chose these words carefully as a synopsis for the book. Of course, the publisher's material and promotion are designed to attract the reader and will be subjective. Now it is up to you to be objective.

3. Read the book (or extracts from most of the sections). Get a feel for the following:

   a. Tone
   b. Style
   c. Readability of the text
   d. Layout
   e. Structure of the content
   f. How it looks
   g. The type of book it is – handbook, manual, how to, autobiography, self-help, practical
   h. Consider what the reader will gain from reading the book
   i. Consider where the book fails, in your opinion
   j. Consider what you like about the book and list the elements that work well
   k. Consider what you feel may have been lacking

      l. Notice the ingredients used by the author – exercises, summaries, cartoons, case studies, anecdotes and so on

      m. Consider the reader to whom you think the book would most appeal

      n. Consider how suitable the author may be as the creator of this book

4. Write the review, according to the required word count, including the most important facts and your byline.

5. Check your review and submit to the editor by email, by the required deadline as an attachment. Include the cover illustration too. Request to be notified when the review is out and get a copy for your files.

6. When your review is out it is nice to notify the publisher of your book. Ask to be kept informed of any new titles.

Sample reviews

Here is a review I just wrote for the 'Expat Living' section of the *Weekly Telegraph*.

Notice how the review is 277 words in length, but that the word count for the whole contribution is 288.

NLP 4 U
Ian Halsall
Lloyd West Publishing
222 pages, paperback, £14 (includes postage)
www.nlp4asia.com

NLP is a hot topic at the moment. Few people remain unaware that this acronym stands for Neuro-Linguistic Programming. Still fewer consider its principles to be bunkum. Ten years ago this Midlands born author discovered that the NLP skills he had learned in the USA worked just as well in his business as in his personal life. So he moved to Asia to teach what he had learned. And there he has remained.

It is hard to come from the Midlands and not be down to earth and Halsall is no exception, which is why his books, and NLP4U is his third book on the subject, are so incredibly easy to read. In short, NLP is the study of human excellence and its tools allow users to get great results. Halsall believes that NLP is not only a fabulous, life-changing tool, but also a skill that is much in demand. Not only is it of benefit to corporations but also in the fields of coaching and mentoring.

This book focuses on how to use NLP to sell things and to persuade others. Skills that we all need regardless of whether we work in a sales environment. Within seconds of completing this book I was able to put what I had learned to good use in a classified advertisement. I will also use its methods to persuade my children to tidy their bedrooms.

This book is practical and while it seems to cover a lot of ground rather fast, this rapid-fire approach is part of its charm. If you are looking for a quick and comprehensive tour of NLP, NLP4U is for you.

Jo Parfitt

288 words

And here are some more samples of my reviews:

Parenting Abroad
Ngaire Jehle-Caitcheon
Aletheia Publications
258 pages, paperback $19.95

The author comes from New Zealand, her husband is Swiss and their two children are real Third Culture Kids who have lived all over the world, surviving war, evacuation and employer bankruptcy. She also has a degree in psychology and a masters in sociology amongst many other qualifications which prove her suitability to write a book of this kind. It is interesting, practical and full of insight, help and support for any expatriate family. This book goes into great detail about how to understand, advise and motivate your children despite upheaval. It will help any parent to cope with such issues as saying goodbye, depression and education and considers each age and stage separately. The author certainly knows her stuff and includes examples and case studies from parents and children all over the world to add authenticity to a book no parent should be without.

Jo Parfitt

157 words

Coaching Across Cultures
Philippe Rosinski
Nicholas Brealey Publishing
314 pages, flexibound, £19.99

Mckinsey and and Deloitte Touche are two companies to have discovered, after much internal research, that the provision of business coaches is one of the best ways to retain and motivate their employees. Yet, today's increasingly global economy dictates that the best coaches should also have the ability to add intercultural understanding to their coaching. Philippe Rosinski can claim to be an expert in the field of coaching across cultures and he was the first continental European to be designated Master Certified Coach by the International Coach Federation. During the last ten years his goal has been to create a coaching model that forms solid bridges not only between cultures, but also between coaching and interculturalism. He is determined that these two professions, coaching and interculturalism, appreciates the importance of the other.

Rosinski's own clients: Unilver, IBM, Baxter Healthcare and Chubb Insurance are proud to be associated with this book and willingly allowed examples from their work with him to be included. Clearly passionate about his topic, the author appears determined to make the reader understand why this matters, where coaching comes from and the huge difference it can make to a business. Throughout the book he provides explanations, techniques and a variety of solutions that he has developed and worked with, such as the Cultural Orientation Framework, teaches the Global Coaching Process and uses the Global Scorecard.

This clearly written book is a serious read. It is thoroughly researched, detailed and fairly academic. It bursts at the seams with examples, diagrams and case studies. Drawing on areas from Transactional Analysis to Neuro Linguistic Programming, it appears that no intercultural stone has been left unturned.

Jo Parfitt

292 words

You can see just some more of my reviews at:

The Weekly Telegraph www.expat.telegraph.co.uk
Enter Asia www.enter-asia.com
Business for Coaches www.businessforcoaches.com

Or just key 'book review Jo Parfitt' into Google for several pages of links!

BONUS TWO

25 Magic Markets for expat writers

The markets listed here may not necessarily pay for your work. They will however, welcome contributions and are a great way for you to practise your pitching, writing and working to deadlines as you build your portfolio.

1) Expatica

www.expatica.com

Expatica has offices in several countries including the Netherlands, Spain, Switzerland, France, Belgium and Germany. Each has its own editor. They look for pieces based on living in each of those countries and tend to be practical and informative.

2) About

www.about.com

Get paid $500 a month in your first year for 12 articles a month on a given a subject.

3) Expat Arrivals

www.expatarrivals.com

This website is always on the look out for articles of use to those about to go abroad or who have just arrived.

4) Paguro

www.paguro.com

Editor, Patrizia Turchetti is keen to have articles on a range of subjects and for a variety of countries. You can even post your own articles here on all aspects of living abroad. They like to use book reviews.

5) I Am Expat

www.iamexpat.nl

Although this website is beginning with the Netherlands it may branch out to include other countries in the future.

6) Tales from a Small Planet

www.talesmag.com

This began as the online magazine for American diplomats overseas and has now expanded to welcome anyone, anywhere. Real Post Reports wanted here about living in specific cities and countries.

7) Helium

www.helium.com

This online magazine takes articles from anyone on any subject

8) Ezine articles

www.ezinearticles.com

This member site will allow you to post your own articles at any time. They may then be used by other websites but you will always get credit for them when they are used.

9) The Telegraph

www.telegraph.co.uk

This Daily Telegraph has an expat living section both in its weekly paper and on its website. It wants pieces of up to 1000 words about expat life. They may also take book reviews and additional content for their website. Good writers may be invited to become regular bloggers for them too. Email the editor of Expat Living on weeklyt@telegraph.co.uk

10) Nexus

www.expatnetwork.com

Editor Sheila Hare Sheila.hare@expatnetwork.com is often on the look out for pieces.

11) Expats

www.expats.org.uk

This site takes articles on a range of subjects of interest to expats.

12) Expatwomen

www.expatwomen.com

Editor Andrea Martins andrea@expatwomen.com is always on the look out for articles, reviews, interviews and much more. She particularly wants interviews with interesting, successful, expat women.

13) Sentinella

www.thesentinella.com

This print magazine is based in Spain and editor, Keidi Keating wants material appropriate to people living on the Costa del Sol. They want book reviews too.

14) Amazing Women Rock

www.amazingwomenrock.com

Susan, the editor of this active website wants stories about amazing women. If you are an amazing woman then you can write your own story too.

15) Expat Daily News

www.expatdailynews.com

This site has morphed out of EscapeArtist and is on the look out for regular correspondents and *ad hoc* articles.

16) Suite 101

www.suite101.com
This website will pay you for articles that adhere to their gudielines if people click on the associated advertising alongside.

17) ExpatExchange

www.expatexchange.com

This site has quite a track record now and is packed with country-specific and general advice on a range of issues to do with living abroad.

18) Living Abroad Magazine

www.livingabroadmagazine.co.uk

This glossy print publication is produced in Scotland and features families who have gone or who are planning to go and live abroad. They pay for pieces, will buy photographs too and like to link to regular bloggers.

19) International Living

www.internationalliving.com

This site has been around for a while and is always on the look out for people to write on a range of subjects. They pay too.

20) Transitions Abroad

www.transitionsabroad.com

Traditionally a publication for young people, students, teachers and backpackers this print magazine likes pieces on exciting and unusual places and projects. They also pay.

21) Examiner

www.examiner.com

A great place for budding writers to place their profile, write regularly and get experience of writing to deadline. There are over 3300 'examiners' around the world, who write about what's on in those countries.

22) ExpatFocus

www.expatfocus.com

This site posts articles by and for expats all over the world.

23) Almerimarlife

www.almerimarlife.com

Chris at Almerimarlife runs an active, interesting online publication, mostly to do with Spain, but he takes general contributions for guest blog posts. Chris is also involved with www.expatsradio.com and may want to interview you too.

24) Expatify

www.expatify.com

This site claims it is turning travellers into expats. It has an extensive list of blogs and its articles, mainly country-specific, receive thousands of views over time.

25) Expat Interviews

www.expatinterviews.com

If you are an expat and live abroad this site may want you to share your story – you can complete their own interview, submit articles or interview other people.

BONUS THREE

Blogging, tweeting and all that jazz

If you are serious about making it as a freelance writer, then I am serious when I tell you that you really should do the following:

- Keep a blog
- Join Twitter
- Set-up Google Alerts

The *blog* will be used to increase your web-presence, to show off your skill and to keep your writing muscles fit and well.

Twitter will be used for you to broadcast the news of all your published articles as and when they appear. It will also be used to help keep you informed of new material and writing and people related to your specialist areas so that you can write about them too.

Google Alerts will alert you to the times that your articles appear online. And will also keep you informed of new material on the Internet associated with your specialism.

Let me explain a bit more about each of these:

Blogging

A blog is a kind of online diary. It was originally called a weblog, and was used to log thoughts, ideas and information on a regular basis.

Today, people are using blogs as an intrinsic part of their social media efforts. Bloggers aim to write interesting, compelling, useful short pieces that readers will love. Then, when they love what you write, they opt to follow all your entries and subscribe to your blog.

If you are forging a career as a writer then blogging is a great way to hone your craft. It will also give you practise in working to deadlines, keeping to a theme and in writing to a certain length.

Blogging is a great boon to the writer because it provides an online showcase that is always active. People comment on the blog entries and sometimes this creates a buzz. When blogs are really popular and brilliantly written this can attract the attention of a publisher who wants to turn the blog into a book. This is what happened to the authors of *Postcards from Across the Pond, Petite Anglaise* and *Julie and Julia*. The main reason people write blogs, newsletters and columns is because they want the reader to start to build a relationship with them. They want to build a tribe, a following and to encourage readers to come back for more. If your goal for writing a blog or column is to build your business then ensure that your posts are all focused on your brand. Try not to be too random.

If you create a blog then, every time you publish a post, you will be found by search engines. The topics in your blog will be found too, and, importantly, this will increase your web presence.

You want editors to feel confident in your ability before they commission you. If you can send them to your active, interesting, well-written blog then they will have hard evidence of your ability.

Setting up a blog

This program is not going to teach you how to set up a blog. You will find plenty of help online and among your blogging friends to give you the assistance you need in setting it up. Instead, I want to emphasise that blogging will boost your online presence in a great way. The more you blog, even if it is only once or twice a month, the more times your name will appear if a potential editor keys your name into a search engine. And that is a good thing.

Your objective, with your blog is threefold:

1   You want 'random' people to find you and sign up to follow your blog.
2   You want a place to post links to everything you have published so this becomes a showcase for your work.
3   You want to increase your Internet presence.

Setting up a blog is free. The most popular are those provided by Wordpress and Blogger. (Please note that both Blogger and Blogspot are the same thing. Blogs that are hosted by Blogger have the URL 'joparfitt.blogspot.com', for example.)

What to blog about

If you want to build a following you need to make a bit of an effort with your blogging. Whatever you post needs to be relevant to you and your work, the brand you are trying to create and the specialism you want people to naturally associate with you.

Just as your business needs to have a clear focus or niche, so too must your blog. If you are too varied you will become nothing to no one and that is no use to you at all.

When you have a niche and a focus you will be easy to remember and easy to refer to potential editors.

Whatever you write needs to be important. There needs to be a point to it, a purpose. Remember the four reasons to write an article? They are the same for a blog. It needs to:

- Inspire
- Support
- Inform
- Entertain

Writing that resonates

See if your writing can really speak to people. Write words that inspire your readers as you share your insights and observations. Writing honestly and with authenticity about your life experiences can help, support and inspire others. This is writing that resonates. This is writing that does more than simply entertain or inform, it makes the reader think differently, see things differently or behave differently as a result. This is writing that lingers in the reader's mind long after she has finished reading. This is writing that people print out and save, forward to their friends and sign up to so they can continue reading more of the same.

If you want to inspire others, this writing is for you. If you want the reader to get a glimpse inside your soul, to see the real you, then you need to write words that resonate. If you want your words to go the extra mile, then this kind of writing is for you. It may be a little close to the bone and personal at times. It may make you feel exposed or vulnerable, but this kind of writing has the potential to change lives.

Ten ideas for writing that resonates

1. Share something personal

2. Expose a weakness, a mistake, an issue

3. Be authentic and honest

4. Be vulnerable

5. Know that your story has the potential to help others

6. Generously share ideas, resources, connections, information, learnings

7. Be meaningful

8. Make the reader think

9. Add value with a link to further information

10. Encourage interaction

How to write words that resonate

- Write in a conversational, chatty tone
- Build a relationship
- Break up your post – use subheads
- Keep it short – 400 words is fine
- Include lots of links to other places or people
- Consider the time of year and write something topical
- End with a question to encourage interaction
- Include lists, top tens, etc
- Add illustrations, videos, podcasts, clips
- When you've written it, share it – Facebook, Twitter etc

The most important thing about a blog is that it is focused. It should help to brand you and increase your reputation as an expert in your specialist fields and as a writer.

Once you have decided on your focus and a name for your blog you need to decide what to write about. Readers like blogs to be personal; here are some ideas for you:

- Amanda van Mulligen's *A Letter From the Netherlands* — http://letterfromthenetherlands.blogspot.com/

- Toni Hargis' *Expat Mum* — http://expatmum.blogspot.com/

- Mike Harling's *Postcards From Across The Pond* — http://postcardsfromacrossthepond.blogspot.com/

Include keywords

Think about what words you key in to a search engine when you are looking for something. Try to use those popular, niche, words in your blog posts, then you will hafe more chance of being found. Interestingly, it is my post on Writing from a Place of Pain, in which I write about being vulnerable, that gets the most hits on my blog. People are searching on the words writing, pain and vulnerable it seems.

Writing lists and tips

Lists and tips work well and appeal to the reader. If you specialise in balcony gardening some of your posts could be on things such as:

- Five ways to make your balcony bloom in winter
- Ten perfect pot plants
- Three little-know watering tips
- Four quotes from wise gardeners

And so on...

Focus

Whatever you write for your blog, remember that a blog is usually short. Many are 400 words or less. Stay focussed in your posts. Stick to one topic and do not allow yourself to digress. If you do have another, albeit connected, idea, be strong and do not let yourself go off at a tangent. Instead, save that post for another post later.

I often say that you can check if you idea has focus if you can describe it in one sentence. The same applies to the blog post.

Linking to other articles

Use your blog to link to all the pieces that you get published online. Simply introduce the topic briefly and then add a link to your article within your blog. The more links you have in your blog entry the better.

Link to your own pieces

I write a monthly column for a local news website. Each month I also link to that post, just as in the one below:

> Back to school. Back to work. Though nature may wind down when autumn creeps in, for writers things really get going. As a writer, September is very probably the best month of all.
>
> Read my column at The Hague Online to find out why.

Link to other people's pieces

If an article by someone else inspires you, then there is no reason why you can't write a short post that then links to that, just as I did here:

> We love our pets, don't we? And many people like to write about theirs. Some, like Barbara Schroeter, choose to write through the eyes of their animals, as done in her dogs' memoir, Gimme One. It is hard to write about pets in a convincing way. It can be easier to be corny than to be compelling. Loving our pets as unconditionally and totally as we do, it is particularly hard to write about them sensitively and yet objectively, particularly when they are ill.
>
> Last week Apple Gidley, aka Expat Apple, did just that, writing about the last days of her family dog. One I am delighted to have known and walked with. An expat dog, who has travelled the world along with her owners.
>
> To read about 'Dog' and witness a superb piece of writing, please go to Apple's blog at the Telegraph and see how to write about a pet without being cheesy.

Link to podcasts and videos

Apparently, links to YouTube videos get more hits than any other kind of blog post. So, see if you can include a variety of media in your blog posts.

Interview people

Stick within your chosen theme or focus but then consider interviewing other people in that field. I feature many expat authors in my blog. The interviews tend to be in the Q&A style, but they can also be proper interviews, or written by the interviewee themselves. If you can record or video some interviews then they could also link to your blog.

Guest posts

Encourage other people, particularly those with active blogs of their own, to write guest posts on your blog. Meanwhile you can offer to guest post on other blogs too. Of course you would write a post on your own blog that links to the place you have guest blogged too! Never miss an opportunity.

News and information

If you are careful to keep abreast of news in your specialist field, then you can write short, sweet blog posts about each item as you hear of it.

Illustrations

Blog posts are always more appealing if they are accompanied by a photograph or image. All blogging software lets you do this easily, so please try to make your blog colourful by adding pictures too.

Links

The more links to other websites and posts and articles that you can have within your post the better. Links act like 'corks' and the more you have the higher up the search engines your posts will come. The fewer links you have the more your posts become like 'stones' and can sink without trace.

How I blog

I am currently blogging three times a week on average. I specialise in expats and writing. That means that I write about people who live abroad, writers who live abroad, people who write books, articles, life story or blogs and I also write about how to write, be inspired and be published (books and articles).

This means that my blog posts tend to cover the following focussed areas:

- Interviews with authors
- Reviews of books by expat authors
- Reviews of books about writing
- Links to great articles by expats or about writing and publishing
- Personal anecdotes that relate to writing, being inspired, writer's block, motivation, self-belief and the other issues experienced by writers
- Links to articles by my students

- Links to articles about me
- Links to other articles by me
- Links to websites that could help my readers
- Links to podcasts
- Links to videos
- Links to interviews
- Further reading and useful resources for expat writers and writers
- News relating to publishing
- Guest posts from other publishing consultants, expat writers and expat authors
- News about upcoming relevant events
- Reports on recent events
- Things I have learned
- Ten Tips
- Seven Secrets
- Six Steps
- And so on

EXERCISE

Take a few moments to complete the following chart:

I think I know a lot about (include areas from your life, work, family, social life):
I have made the following mistakes and learned from them:
I could share top tips about the following:

At this time of year I could write about my thoughts on:

I follow these websites to keep me informed about news and events in my specialist field:

I could interview the following people:

I could create podcasts and video on the following:

Using Twitter

Twitter is a micro-blogging tool. It allows you to write mini posts of up to just 140 characters each. Just as you want people to follow your blog posts, you also want to encourage people to follow your Tweets.

As a writer you need to join Twitter and create a Twittername that is memorable and easy to type. Expatwriter, WriterinHolland, JordanJourno perhaps, or just your name.

You will need to upload an image too, so that people will recognise you.

This is my current image. I paid a professional photographer to take the photograph because I wanted to use one that was a good reflection of me and my work. A photo of me at a party, holding a wine glass would not have helped my business.

Millions of people use Twitter and the more active members follow over a thousand other Twitterers and are followed by as many people themselves.

As a writer, you will be using Twitter to meet people who could feature in your writing, and to find markets for your work, places to guest post, magazines and websites.

You will also use it to source news, information and articles you can write about.

And, you will post a Tweet every time you make a blog post or get published online too.

You can set up your Facebook and Linked In accounts to automatically post your Twitter updates there too and this will expand the reach of your Tweets.

What to tweet about

You will want to tweet about things that are related to your brand as a writer. If you specialise in property development then you would tweet links to articles, news, people, posts and other information to do with this area.

Tweets need to be valuable and compelling and, to my mind, the best ones ask the viewer to do something – usually click on a link within the Tweet that will take them to another website, your website or your blog. When you key a long URL into Twitter it will automatically be shortened. This is pretty important when you consider that you only have 140 characters to use.

You can ask a question in your Tweets too. Once, when my email program stopped working I tweeted for help and within minutes a range of complete strangers had come to my aid.

Use keywords in your Tweets so that other people who are interested in those areas will find your Tweets. So, if you are interesting in expat or overseas issues, you should include those words as often as possible.

What to include

Just as you need to include special keywords in your blog posts so that people will find you via search engines, so too do you need to do that with your Tweets.

I work with free software called Tweetdeck rather than Twitter (there are many other popular alternatives out there too, including Hootsuite), and it allows me to add columns that permanently search on specific words that are important to me. So, I have a column for the word *expat* and one for the word *write*. This means that I can see every other tweet including those words and that alerts me to useful people I may like to follow, other articles and websites I may need to know about and so on.

It can be good to include the names of other Twitterers in your Tweets too. You do this by adding their name preceded by the @ symbol. When you include the Twittername of someone else in your Tweet this is called a *mention*. Mentioning other people will encourage them to mention you in return.

174

Try to mention people who can support you and whose content will also be of interest to your followers.

Retweeting

It is common to resend Tweets, send by someone else, out to your own list of followers. This is called Retweeting (RT). Retweeting is a good way to *mention* people. So, when expat author, Carolyn Vines, known as @blackandabroad, published her new memoir, called *Black and (A)broad*, I was quick to mention it, that and the fact that she was my client. My aim was a) to tell people that I had a client b) to tell people my client was successful c) to send them to my blog where I had more information d) let Carolyn know I had *mentioned* her. Often when you mention people they will be keen to send that same message to their followers too.

This was my message:

"Congrats to my client @blackandabroad on the publication of her new memoir Black and (A)broad. See our interview at http://www.xxx.xxx"

When Carolyn Retweeted it she wrote:

"Thx to @joparfitt for the RT about publication of my memoir Black and (A)broad. See our interview at http://www.xxx.xxx"

Many people take Retweeting, known as RTing, to the extreme, putting collections of Twitternames together on a Friday, known as a Follow Friday or #FF. Follow Friday tweets indicate people you like and who you follow. Wednesdays are Writers Wednesday or #WW.

Hashtags

The hashtag or # is used, for common words used in Twitter. You can find lists of hashtags online so that you can be sure to use the standard ones and not simply make up your own. Commonly, hashtags are used in conjunction with abbreviations, see #WW and #FF, above. It makes the abbreviation easier to find. A local business group, called the Women's Business Initiative International, has the Twitter name @WBII, but when it is also known by the hashtag #WBII.

If I want to really flag up the words in my own Tweets that I want others to notice, I could use a hashtag. So, this means I would use #write and #expat for example.

Examples of Tweets

Your Tweets should be used to promote your skill, your specialism and your published writing. Here are some possible ideas for Tweets that would achieve this for you:

"Read my expat blog about moving to Spain with a dachsund here http://xxx.xxx"

"10 tips for overseas wardrobe weeders here http://xxx.xxx"

"Life coaching secrets for expats from the world's celebrity coaches here http://xxx.xxx"

"See my latest article at @Iamexpat, about buying bulbs, at http://xxx.xxx"

And so on...

Remember your goal as a new writer is to let people know about your blog posts and articles that appear online, to flag your success stories and to become known for your specialism. Ensure your Tweets relate to your objective and, when possible, lead people to a link to an article or to your blog.

Google Alerts

In order to keep a check on how many times your name is appearing on the Internet you should sign up with the free Google Alert service from Google at www.google.com/alerts.

Simply ask to be notified by email whenever the words you want to look for appear online and the alerts will appear in your inbox.

I have set up to be alerted whenever my name appears, the word 'expat' and also my specialisms of 'life story' and 'portable careers'. These last three alerts help to keep me informed of new developments and websites.

Social media for writers

Social media is a fantastic, free marketing tool and you need to use it. Start off with a blog, Twitter and some alerts and see how this affects your writing business.

Over time, you can add Linked In, Facebook and other platforms, such as Digg, Delicious, Stumble-Upon, YouTube and Tumblr to the mix and start to embrace the opportunities they provide.

BONUS FOUR

Podcast 'So, You Want To Write Articles?'

The fourth and final bonus that you receive along with this course is an audio recording that I made that will outline the most important points about writing and selling articles.

You can listen to yours at the link below:

www.joparfitt.com/mp3.html

Lightning Source UK Ltd.
Milton Keynes UK
UKOC01f0910130813

215150UK00002B/3/P